W9-CYN-108

AMERICAN OPINION
ON WORLD AFFAIRS
IN THE ATOMIC AGE

BASED ON A REPORT PREPARED FOR THE
COMMITTEE ON THE SOCIAL AND ECONOMIC ASPECTS
OF ATOMIC ENERGY
OF THE
SOCIAL SCIENCE RESEARCH COUNCIL

AMERICAN OPINION
ON WORLD AFFAIRS
IN THE ATOMIC AGE

By LEONARD S. COTTRELL, JR.,

& SYLVIA EBERHART

With a Foreword by FREDERICK OSBORN, Deputy U.S.
Representative, UN Atomic Energy Commission

GREENWOOD PRESS, PUBLISHERS
NEW YORK

FOREWORD

EVEN the high level of leadership now given us by Secretary of State Marshall will be ineffective unless our policies are carried out in a manner acceptable to public opinion. Public opinion surveys, for all their weaknesses and need of interpretation, provide the only available means of factual information in this vital field.

This book is a summary of a study of American attitudes toward foreign affairs, especially in relation to atomic energy. Although presumably it will be read chiefly by those interested and well-informed, it still seems worth while to summarize in this foreword the best present views on the significance of atomic energy, what atomic energy is, and the progress of negotiations for its control.

Atomic energy has significance for the human race because it can produce explosions of unprecedented violence, whose aftermath may destroy life in large areas. It thus raises the vital question whether the world as a whole is civilized enough to stay alive under these new circumstances.

Atomic energy will also become a source of power. But it will not greatly reduce the cost of power in any large-scale substitution for present fuels, and it will probably be many years before it finds even a limited use in this field.

The scientific interest in atomic energy is considerable, for it opens up an entirely new field of discovery. Its use in science is as a technical tool for conducting experiments, which may lead to a further great increase in our knowledge of the physical and biological world. To the layman this may seem dangerous, unless accompanied by a corresponding increase in social controls.

Having thus briefly outlined what appears to be the significance of atomic energy, I feel it will be worth while to refresh our memories as to what atomic energy is, what it comes from, and the present state of the negotiations for its international control.

At present atomic energy comes from one of three heavy metals. These metals are uranium 235, plutonium, and uranium 233. They are very expensive to make. Their production involves a period of time, measured in years rather than in months, and large complicated plants. Plutonium and uranium 233 do not occur in nature, and uranium 235 occurs only in small quantities and is hard to extract. These three metals are in many ways similar to ordinary metals. But, given the proper mechanism to set them off, they will explode with a violence many thousands of times greater than that of dynamite or TNT. Given another kind of mechanism, they can be made to give off heat more slowly and without an explosion. Scientists and engineers believe that this heat can be extracted so as to make it a useful source of power. It cannot be done now, and may never be done economically enough for large-scale use, because we haven't the necessary engineering knowledge or the necessary types of materials. Nevertheless, because these metals have tremendous power to give off heat, they are called nuclear fuels.

Most industrial nations already know the major principles involved in making nuclear fuel. But to put these fuels to effective use involves an advanced technology and great expense. In time they will learn how to make effective bombs. Whether they can make them in quantity is another matter. If all nations went ahead to develop nuclear fuels—just as they do other resources, such as coal and water power—they would not only be preparing to produce atomic power, but they would also soon have on hand a stock of explosives enough to destroy a large part of the world's population. You can see it wouldn't be a very safe world to live in. That is the reason the United States has urged international control and a single international agency responsible for all large-scale atomic energy activities. Otherwise, it is likely that nations would stock up on nuclear fuel, pretending that they were going to use it to make power, but always with the danger that they were going to use it for explosives in a war.

The dangers of such a world would bear hardest on the democracies. No democratic country would be likely to plan an aggressive war, to be opened with a surprise attack by atomic weapons. For the democracy, the atomic bomb would be a weapon of defense and counterattack. For the police state, the atomic bomb would be a weapon of propaganda, a great asset in the war of nerves, and it might even give, in practice, a considerable advantage at the start of a war. But it is likely that the fear of effective retaliation by a nation with as many or more bombs would be a strong deterrent to such an act of aggression. Even if the Soviet Union should develop bombs, as it has announced its intention of doing, there is no reason why the United States should not retain its lead in this field, until a plan for effective international control is accepted by the U.S.S.R. There can be no doubt of the ability of the United States to maintain such a lead if it deems it necessary.

Twelve nations are represented on the Atomic Energy Commission, which was created by the General Assembly of the United Nations in January 1946. Ten of them have agreed that once a fully effective system of control is established, no nation should any longer have atomic bombs. But the Soviet Union and Poland insist that the United States must destroy all its atomic bombs before any system of control is in operation. This the United States has refused to do. Moreover, the Soviet Union and Poland have a very different view as to what controls are required. The Commission has been working for more than a year, and the majority have written and voted for two reports to the Security Council. The First Report, made in December 1946, lays out the general principles of a treaty to control atomic energy, and the Second Report, submitted in September 1947, lays out in detail the functions of the international agency which would be set up under such a treaty. The Commission proposes that the international agency should have control of all dangerous activities involving nuclear fuels, commencing with the ownership by the international agency of the ores when they are taken out of the ground and continuing with the ownership, management, and operation of all dangerous facilities by the agency. Nuclear fuels would be produced only when they were actually needed for peaceful purposes. All atomic weapons would be disposed of. World security against atomic warfare is what we are looking for. If and when atomic power becomes practical, power would be made available to all nations on a fair basis, if the conditions of world security then make it possible. Meanwhile, research with nondangerous quantities, for peaceful purposes, would be permitted to nations and peoples all over the world, under suitable controls. There would be a complete exchange of information and no longer any secrets among scientists in this field. At the same time, the agency would carry on a system of inspection of all countries to make sure that no nation was carrying on clandestine activities of a dangerous sort.

The Soviet Union abstained from voting on the First Report to the Security Council, and voted against the Second Report. The Soviets have made alternative proposals. They propose to let every country go ahead with its own develop-

ment of nuclear fuels on some system of exploitation laid out
in a treaty and subject only to some kind of inspection by an
international agency which would, in the words of the Soviet
Union's proposal, make recommendations to each country
and make recommendations to the Security Council, where
action would be subject to veto. The Soviet Union and Poland
say that this would be a sufficient control. The majority say
that it is not a sufficient control, that it would lead to national
rivalries and to the danger of an atomic war. So the Atomic
Energy Commission is deadlocked. The Soviet Union says
that there is no possibility of reaching agreement unless the
majority come around to the views of the Soviets. The majority say no agreement can be reached unless the Soviet Union
comes around to the views of the majority. There can be no
middle ground on the functions of the international agency,
if effective control is the goal. There does not seem to be
any real compromise possible between a system under which
the agency would own, operate, and manage all dangerous
facilities and a system under which governments would own,
operate, and manage all dangerous facilities, with an international agency making inspections and recommendations.
The United States made an offer unprecedented in the history of the world when it proposed to give up atomic bombs,
provided that a real system of control were set up to make sure
that no other nation would make them. That offer still stands.

The behavior of the Soviets in the Atomic Energy Commission raises the question whether the Soviet Union will
agree to any effective scheme for the control of atomic energy
unless and until its foreign policy takes a very different form
from that which it has at present. A really effective control
would require a degree of international cooperation which
the Soviets may feel is incompatible with the theory of an
ultimate and inevitable conflict between "Communism" and

"Capitalism," incompatible with the Iron Curtain, and incompatible with their present spirit of suspicion and noncooperation. Some day in the future, when the economy of Europe is restored, it is likely that the Soviet Union may be forced to rearrange its approach to international affairs in order that its own people may share in the economic improvement attained in other countries. At such a time the Soviets may weigh their undoubted dislike of the fact that the United States has a preponderance of atomic weapons and the means of delivering them, against their dislike of a system of inspection which would break down the Iron Curtain. If such a day should come, effective international control of atomic energy and its use for peaceful purposes alone would again become a possibility.

This survey of American opinion concerning atomic energy is important because it provides the fullest and most systematic report that we have yet had concerning how the people of this country feel about the atomic bomb. To those of us concerned daily with negotiating for international control of atomic energy, the findings of the survey are particularly significant. There are apparently still many citizens who are very poorly informed about the fundamental facts of atomic energy control. The survey was made a year after the United Nations was established, yet a third of the people interviewed could not explain, even in general terms, the purposes of the United Nations. In August 1946, according to the findings of the survey, two percent of the American people had never heard of the atomic bomb. The percentage is not large, but it seems hard to believe that after all the efforts to enlighten the public there may still be some two million people in this country who have never heard of the bomb. Even among those who are relatively well-informed, there is a group that might be classified as the nonworriers—those who take the view that there is no use worrying about something you can't help.

Atomic energy raises so many new problems that an unprecedented degree of thought and understanding is called for from people in all parts of the world. The United States has taken the lead in providing the basic facts essential to understanding the problem. It provided the basis for a plan that would make international controls effective and that, with modifications introduced by other delegations, took form in the First and Second Reports of the Atomic Energy Commission. These reports were approved by all the nations participating in the negotiations of the Commission except Poland and the Soviet Union.

World-wide opinion supporting effective control can best be based upon knowledge of the facts. The debate on atomic energy is only a part of the greater debate which is going on all over the world and in which the United States and the Soviet Union are the major protagonists. If we can win this debate we will have no war. But if we fail to win enough people to our side, our civilization may well go down in the attempt to defend it with arms. This debate is not carried on by the Soviets with objective logic. The idea that the welfare of the common man can best be protected by a police state, ruled by the iron hand of a self-perpetuating dictatorship, is not an idea which can be maintained in any debate in which objective truth or the experience of history play a part. The Soviet argument is, therefore, largely emotional. It sows confusion and distrust, invites recriminations, provides scapegoats, draws red herrings across the trail of constructive effort. Our method must be the truth, based on the use of carefully determined objective facts which lie behind all the great issues separating the Soviet Union from the rest of the world.

In the long run, we must believe that the objective facts will overcome the emotional appeal. Otherwise, we would lose all hope for the intelligent direction of human affairs. But for the shorter term, the Soviet appeal must seem to them to have certain advantages.

We must remember that three-fourths of the people of this globe are quite uneducated, terribly poor, and wholly inexperienced in any part of the Western European tradition —whether its religious tradition of the integrity of the individual, its political tradition, or its tradition of thinking based on objective facts. The great majority of the people of the world have never known anything except an authoritarian form of government. We may believe that the truth will prevail, but it is evident that under these conditions it will take a long time.

Perhaps it is fortunate that the Soviets are forcing this debate upon us with all the power and energy at their command. We, in turn, are obliged to look to our own moral and intellectual forces to reappraise and to argue, with all the strength of which we are capable, the tradition of the free man, for the defense of which we are now so largely responsible. Perhaps it is only by being faced with such desperate necessity that we can obtain that rededication to the truth, without which the truth would perish.

Unfortunately, the word "truth," when it refers to any matter concerned with human affairs, is too often, or even necessarily, only a subjective affirmation. Even the "experience of history" is subject to different interpretations according to the personal biases of the interpreter. All these great truths which we hold to be self-evident are, in effect, working hypotheses. We are justified in holding to them more or less firmly in proportion as we have facts or objective data to support them. The progress of modern social thinking depends on the progress we are able to make in developing new techniques, new methods of analysis of factual objective data. In our war of words with the Soviet Union we are as dependent on the development of tools and mechanisms as in any physical war. The public opinion survey is such a tool.

The public opinion survey itself gives no final answers. It still requires to be analyzed by experts. Questions of depth or intensity or persistence of attitudes among a small number of people may be even more important than the attitude of a majority at any given time. The present volume makes these difficulties clear and is thus of particular value to the layman who properly tends to approach a new technique with caution. But as the techniques of such studies and their interpretation improve, this new instrument will increasingly give us a background of fact against which to check on the validity of the hypotheses or assumptions which are a necessary premise to practical action.

This volume marks, then, a new approach to the study of human as well as international affairs. Read in that light, it acquires an importance transcending even the urgent matters with which it deals.

February 1, 1948   FREDERICK OSBORN
                                    Deputy U.S. Representative
                                    U.N. Atomic Energy Commission

AUTHORS' PREFACE

IN RECOGNITION of the critical importance of more adequate knowledge of the thinking of the American public on matters relating to the development of the atomic bomb and its effect on attitudes on international relations, the Committee on Social Aspects of Atomic Energy of the Social Science Research Council, under the chairmanship of Winfield Riefler, proposed early in 1946 that a study of public opinion and attitudes in these areas be undertaken. At the request of the above-named committee, a subcommittee composed of Hadley Cantril, Pendleton Herring, Rensis Likert, and Leonard S. Cottrell, Jr., Chairman, accepted responsibility for planning and supervising the proposed study.

Upon recommendation of the subcommittee, Cornell University applied for grants of $23,875 each from the Carnegie Corporation of New York and the Rockefeller Foundation for the conduct of the study. The chairman of the subcommittee was asked to assume general administrative direction of the project.

In view of the proposed atomic bomb experiment at Bikini, it was agreed that the project should include surveys of opinions and attitudes before and after the Bikini experiment. This plan made it possible to determine not only what the prevailing opinions and attitudes were among various segments of the American public but also the extent of the changes which might occur following the naval experiment. It was recognized, of course, that it would not be possible to attribute causal significance to that experiment alone since other events

xv

would be occurring during the same time interval which could also have an effect on opinion. As it turned out, there were no important changes in opinion resulting from the experiment so far as this study could determine.

In order to utilize both extensive or polling methods and intensive methods of opinion and attitude research, the subcommittee decided to conduct two surveys simultaneously before and after the Bikini Operation. One survey was designed to utilize the extensive methods used by the American Institute of Public Opinion and other similar opinion polling agencies. The other survey was designed to utilize the more intensive interviewing methods developed by Rensis Likert and his associates. Both surveys were based on national cross-section samples questioned before the bomb test, and comparable samples surveyed after the test.

The extensive or polling surveys used the quota method of sampling and formal questionnaires which called for responses to questions in fixed-answer categories. This method permitted the collection of data from larger samples, although fewer questions could be asked of each respondent than was true in the case of the intensive surveys. A total of approximately 6000 respondents were included in the extensive survey samples (approximately 3000 each in the "before" and "after" surveys).

The intensive surveys used an area sampling procedure. The interview plan permitted a more informal response and allowed many more topics to be covered than did the polling questionnaire. Moreover, the interview was designed to obtain more data by more "probing" into the reasoning which lay behind the subject's responses. A total of approximately 1200 cases were included in the sample, 600 before and 600 after the bomb tests.

A detailed report of the methods and findings of the surveys mentioned above was published by Cornell University in April 1947, entitled *Public Reaction to the Atomic Bomb and World Affairs*. It contains a report of the extensive surveys prepared by Richard S. Crutchfield of Swarthmore College and a report of the intensive surveys prepared by Angus Campbell, Sylvia Eberhart, and Patricia Woodward of the Survey Research Center of the University of Michigan.

This book, based primarily on the two aforementioned reports, is essentially an interpretation of the significant findings of the whole study. It is written primarily for the intelligent citizen who is interested in knowing what important facts the surveys reveal about the thinking of his fellow citizens and the significance of these facts for the American public, confronted as it is by the necessity of participating in decisions of incalculable importance to our common future.

With this purpose in mind, the authors have naturally omitted many of the detailed findings and have reduced technical discussions to a minimum.* Moreover they have had to take the responsibility for judging what the important findings are and for interpreting the significance of these findings. In doing this they have had to go beyond the functions of merely reporting the answers Americans have given to questions on the issues involved, and have attempted to provide an understanding of the American state of mind or manner of thinking on these issues and to point out some of the implications of this way of thinking. The more critical reader who prefers not to depend upon the interpretation of the authors is of course invited to refer to the detailed report of findings, which he may interpret for himself.

It is hardly necessary to say that no one connected with this

* The Appendix of this book contains the tabulations on which most of the figures given in the text are based. However, references are not made in the text to page numbers or table numbers in the Appendix since these would be so numerous that they would interfere with readability.

project regards the findings or interpretation as the final word on American reaction to the problems raised by the atom bomb. Time and events change opinions and ways of thinking. More intensive research reveals more facets of a problem. We do hold, however, that this report serves as a worth-while beginning and expect it to be the stimulus and point of departure for further studies of the problem.

The subcommittee and the authors wish at this time gratefully to acknowledge the contributions made to this project by many agencies and persons. The Social Science Research Council Committee on Social Aspects of Atomic Energy gave the impetus to the study. The Carnegie Corporation of New York and the Rockefeller Foundation made the project possible by their generous grants of funds. Cornell University sponsored the research and made its administrative services and facilities available to us. We are indebted to Benson and Benson, Inc., of Princeton, New Jersey, for the field work on the extensive surveys and to Richard S. Crutchfield for his analysis and report of those surveys. Similarly, acknowledgments are due to the staff of the Survey Research Center of the University of Michigan for the field work and analysis on the intensive surveys.

We desire also to thank the following for permission to quote from their surveys: The National Opinion Research Center (formerly at the University of Denver, now at the University of Chicago); the American Institute of Public Opinion (Gallup Poll); Elmo Roper; the editors of *Fortune*; the Iowa Poll; and the Survey Research Center at the University of Michigan. For permission to quote from their books or manuscripts, we wish to thank Hadley Cantril, and John Wiley and Sons, Publishers; Jerome S. Bruner, and Duell, Sloan and Pearce, Publishers; and Dorwin Cartwright.

Many persons have made valuable contributions to various

phases of this work. Special thanks are due Frederick Osborn for his Foreword to this book; to Angus Campbell, Patricia Woodward, Lloyd A. Free and Louis Guttman for their assistance at several stages of the work of planning and analysis; to Meta F. Cooper, Anne Christopher and Carolyn Gavlin for their careful and efficient help in various administrative phases of the project; and to Charles Dollard and Donald Young for their wise and sympathetic counsel throughout the study.

LEONARD S. COTTRELL, JR.

SYLVIA EBERHART

February 1, 1948

CONTENTS

AMERICAN OPINION
ON WORLD AFFAIRS
IN THE ATOMIC AGE

CHAPTER I · "ISSUES" AND PUBLIC OPINION

IF "PUBLIC OPINION" suggests simply a tally of pro's and con's on "issues," then it is a misnomer for what we shall attempt to describe in this book. As a consequence of a rather general and perhaps natural oversimplification, public opinion polls have come to be looked upon as plebiscites expressing the "will" of the people. On the one hand, poll results may be pointed to by political pressure groups—and others—as mandates from the people, which presumably no official of a democratic government dares disregard. On the other hand, polls have been decried as dangerous or as nuisances by those who, while accepting them as evidences of the popular will, believe the people to be unfit to render judgment on public issues. The first appraisal may at times harass responsible officials. The second embarrasses our belief that popular participation in government is an essential feature of democracy.

It is true that at the same time that some polls are offered as representing the votes of the people on grave and difficult issues, other polls reveal the people's ignorance of even elementary facts about their country's political institutions. For example, at least a third of the people appear never to have heard of the Bill of Rights, and only a fifth can explain what it is; and half the people do not know that members of the House of Representatives are elected to two-year terms. But the error here is not in attaching significance to public opinion; it is rather in assuming that public opinion must function as a directive. We do not have, and it is not likely that we could have, in our complex civilization, government by plebiscite. Moreover, considering practically how an unofficial poll functions, it is clear that there must be a critical difference between—on the one hand—going voluntarily to an official polling place, at the conclusion of a highly organized campaign, and casting a vote with a consciousness of participating in government, and —on the other hand—replying to a poll-taker who comes unexpectedly to the door to ask a question to which one may or may not have given any previous thought. It is unreasonable indignantly to charge the people with being unfit to determine the solution of specific governmental problems when they have not, in fact, assumed the responsibility for doing so.

Yet the people's wishes and beliefs do stand in some relation, and often a critical relation, to public policies on which they may never be called upon to cast an official vote. (Witness their role in the Treasury's wartime anti-inflationary policy, to take an obvious example.) Not only elected representatives but nonelective public administrators strive continually to gauge and understand public feeling. As one social psychologist whose public opinion research had very practical wartime purposes puts it: "Looking at the government through the eyes of those who shape policies . . . it is not enough to know whether or not the public is in favor of some broadly defined program. . . . Even though the objectives receive overwhelming approval, a program may fail because its detailed operation does not correctly take into account the 'human element' inherent in any public action." [1]

David E. Lilienthal has described the problems of controlling atomic energy and preventing its use for destruction as a problem calling for "the scientific spirit and the scientific method" rather than "the political method." But he has also

[1] Dorwin Cartwright, "Public Opinion Polls and Democratic Leadership," *Journal of Social Issues*, May 1946.

urged that the people's frame of mind may well become a critical factor in determining whether the desirable solutions to that problem are allowed to prevail. "It is my opinion," he said in a recent address, "that we cannot make wise decisions in this country respecting this great and staggering discovery and its future use for peace and security unless the citizenry of the country does have an understanding of the fundamental facts and an understanding of the potentialities and realities of this discovery that we call atomic energy." [2] This statement voices the concern that many scientists, government officials, and military men now have about what the people are thinking regarding the issues involved.

The Purpose of This Book

A better term than "opinion" for what we shall try to deal with is, perhaps, "frame of mind." We shall examine not only which of several alternatives people choose in answering questions about the atomic bomb and about the international problems posed by the bomb, but also, so far as we can, the reasons why they think as they do. We shall try to discover how deeply concerned the people are about the atomic bomb, and how well-aware they are of the issues it has raised. We shall see what light is thrown by opinion surveys on the values or beliefs, the fears or misgivings, that arise in people's minds when they think about control of the bomb and about the role of the United States in the world.

Most of the findings come from two surveys—an "extensive" survey, or poll, and an "intensive" survey—conducted in the summer of 1946 upon the recommendation of the Committee on the Social Aspects of Atomic Energy, of the Social Science

[2] Statement made before a meeting of the Inland Daily Press Association in Chicago, May 26, 1947.

Research Council.[3] The general nature of a public opinion poll is probably fairly well-known to most newspaper readers. It consists of asking one or more questions of a large and representative sample of the population. These questions are so designed that the answers can be fitted by the poll-taker into a few predetermined categories and then easily tallied. The advantage of this kind of survey, by comparison with the intensive survey, is that its much lower unit cost makes practicable the polling of a larger sample and therefore a wider range of statistical manipulation.

The intensive survey is a somewhat newer development, and not so well-known outside professional circles. It is conducted by means of lengthy, detailed interviews with a relatively small, although representative, sample of the people.[4] The interviewer is armed with a long series of questions which have been designed with the purpose of stimulating an informal conversation, in the course of which the person being interviewed will not only state his opinions but will explain them in his own way. Many of the questions are "open"—that is, instead of being asked to choose from a number of stated alternatives, the respondent is asked to give his own free answer, based on what he himself sees to be the alternatives.[5] The interviewer's task is to encourage the respondent to enlarge on his answers, particularly by asking him, "Why do you think so?" but without in any way influencing the respondent's reasoning. The respondent's answers and comments are written down by the interviewer as nearly verbatim as possible; there are no checklists or predetermined categories

[3] The survey findings are reported in detail in a 300-page lithoprinted volume, *Public Reaction to the Atomic Bomb and World Affairs*, published by Cornell University, April 1947.

[4] Regarding the samples drawn for the surveys upon which this book is based, see Appendix B.

[5] Verbatim reports of illustrative interviews are included in Appendix A.

of answers for the interviewer to check. (Thus, if the respondent's initial answer to a question is, "Yes, I certainly think
so, because . . . ," it remains distinguishable from the answer
of another respondent who may say only, "Well, I guess so.")
The verbatim records so gathered are then assembled for
detailed analysis by a specially trained staff.

With insight into what underlies the opinions people express, their answers to any single question may take on a
new significance. Suppose we ask the respondent, "How do
you feel about bringing down tariffs?" He answers, "Why,
I don't think we ought to bring them down. Tariffs should
be high, in order to protect our standard of living." His
vote, apparently, is cast in favor of high tariffs. Then suppose
we continue with this question: "Some feel we should keep
our tariffs high to keep out foreign goods, even if that means
we sell less of our goods to foreign countries. What do you
think about that?" He may then answer, "Well, they should
be high enough to protect our standard of living. But of
course they needn't be so high that they cut down foreign
trade. Foreign trade is valuable to our country." [6]
It might be argued that we should have asked him the
second, more informative, question in the first place—in which
case he would probably have cast the opposite vote. But this
argument is of doubtful value if our object is to find out what
is the man's frame of mind on the subject. His reaction to the
first question—especially when checked against his reaction
to the second—suggests that he cannot have been much aware
of a tariff *issue*. We have learned that he has some predisposi-
tion to react favorably to the idea of high tariffs, when they are
mentioned, because there is a relation in his mind between them
and a desirable standard of living. It is necessary to remind him

[6] The example is taken by permission from an actual survey interview of
the Survey Research Center, University of Michigan.

of the connection between tariffs and foreign trade. This reminder at once causes something of a shift in his position, because he also reacts unfavorably to the idea of reducing foreign trade, having an appreciation of the connection between buying from abroad and selling abroad. His final position appears to be that we should do about tariffs whatever has to be done to protect our standard of living *and* to encourage foreign trade. If this is the question at issue, it is hardly fair to represent him as having cast a vote on that issue. Many such survey questions, even on much better publicized issues, are not seen by most people as issue-questions at all. Unless people are rather specifically aware of the current and actual problem represented, they will not identify the survey question with a specific issue. They will react simply according to the general values or principles the question seems to them to represent.

Thus, we would undoubtedly find people generally reacting favorably to the idea that the government should do everything it can to stimulate world trade. May we infer from this that they will react favorably to the proposal of extending large credits to Great Britain? We find, when we ask them what they think of a proposed loan to Britain, that the majority react unfavorably. Examples could be multiplied almost endlessly from the files of public opinion surveys to show that the reactions to a proposal made in general terms differ widely from reactions to what is essentially the same proposal made in specific terms. It seems obvious that in order to appraise people's reactions either to a general proposition (the desirability of stimulating world trade) or to a concrete proposal (the British loan) we must seek some insight into their understanding of these questions. When they agree that stimulating world trade is a good thing, have they any notion of what must be done to accomplish this end? When they express disapproval of the British loan, do they oppose it as a measure to stimulate world trade? Moreover, even when they favor the British loan, are they favoring it because they look on it as a measure to stimulate world trade, or because they like Great Britain and tend to favor any measure expressive of friendliness to her? After exploring these questions, we may come to the conclusion that the people's opinions about the British loan stem from the inadequacy of their information about its purposes and their low level of understanding of the economics of a foreign loan.

But even this statement may only partly represent the people's frame of mind. It leaves open the question, how much are they concerned about the issue? Will they really pay much attention to the government's course of action? Will they experience a sense of satisfaction if the government acts in conformity with the opinion they have expressed, or a sense of indignation if it does not? In other words, how much interest and conviction lie behind their responses?

The question of interest, conviction, and concern is an especially important one in connection with the issues the development of the atomic bomb has raised. The responsibility for finding solutions to the problems raised by the atomic bomb belongs, as Mr. Lilienthal has indicated, to experts, not to the citizenry. But it is at least thinkable that the extent to which the people's representatives feel the urgency of accepting such solutions and putting them to work in spite of the differences and difficulties that will inevitably arise may depend in large measure upon public concern.

"What People?"

In general parlance, the word "public" in "public opinion" may mean some segment, defined or undefined, of the population—the "informed" public, the most vocal members of an elected official's constituency, the public represented by organizations, the kind of people with whom the speaker has some contact or whose opinions he esteems, etc. In public opinion polls and surveys, however, "public" means usually the entire adult population.[7] While all survey organizations are not yet agreed on what techniques constitute the best sampling method, the reputable organizations all strive to attain as nearly perfect "representative cross-sections" as possible, with a striking degree of success.

This fact may raise the question, but do all the people count, so far as public opinion is concerned—even the totally indifferent, the uneducated, those who never bother to vote? The answer can only be that indifference, disparities in education, and variations in sense of social responsibility are facts of our political life that exercise their own influences. Certainly each person's opinions or preferences do not exercise the same force. Nor is any given individual or group as influential for some issues or circumstances as for others. But the opinion surveys have taken as their province the study of the public as a whole, not the study of "pressures" or special influences, which manifest themselves directly and are in themselves major areas of investigation. It is frequently valuable to single out the opinions of some one segment of the population for study, and in cross-section surveys a standard method of analysis is to divide the sample according to various criteria— amount of formal schooling, income bracket, occupation, etc. —in order to see whether segments of the population differ from each other in attitude, and how they differ. It is often useful to observe on a particular question that even though no one opinion is held by a majority of all the people, one opinion does predominate among those who express opinions. But the proportion of people who express no opinion on a given issue is of itself often a major finding, for it varies greatly from issue to issue and is therefore often a partial indicator of the current level of information about or interest in the particular question.

How opinions relate to level of information and understanding is as a rule a matter of special interest. This is usually represented in the reports of surveys by dividing respondents into educational groups—those who have little or no formal schooling, those who have had high-school education, those who have been to college. In our two surveys, an attempt was made to appraise directly each respondent's level of information about world affairs, and in the findings described in this book we refer from time to time to "well-informed" and "less well-informed" or "poorly informed" people.[8] It must be explained that these are relative, not absolute, terms. That is, those to whom we refer as well-informed showed themselves in certain ways to be better informed than the others about current affairs. In the extensive survey, respondents were asked a series of questions of fact about the atomic bomb and about events and persons then very much in the news. The respondents were later classified on a seven-point scale according to the accuracy of their answers. In the intensive survey, respondents were classified as having a low level of information if they appeared not to know what was meant by "United Nations organization," "atomic bomb," "England," or "Russia." Their informational level was considered "medium" if they understood these terms, but failed to indicate any specific information that would qualify them for the highest rating. It was considered "high" if during the course of the interview they made any specific reference to places where events of importance had recently occurred (Iran, Palestine, Argentina,

[8] See Appendix B for tabulations.

India, etc.), to persons prominent in world affairs, other than President Truman (Churchill, Gromyko, Molotov, Bevin, Byrnes), or to events or issues being currently discussed (the Russian representatives' "walking out" of UN meetings, the question of Russian troops in Iran, the resignation of Secretary Stettinius, the veto power in the UN, the Baruch plan, etc.). These procedures proved highly satisfactory for sorting individuals into broad categories, but it is obvious that although those who are accordingly classified as "well-informed" are as a group better informed than the others, they do not necessarily meet some desired standard of excellence. The three-point scale of the intensive survey was found to divide the sample roughly into thirds. The seven-point scale classified 16 percent of the people at the very bottom, eight percent at the top, and from 12 to 20 percent at each of the intervening points.

The correlations between attitudes or opinions and level of information of course resembled those between attitudes or opinions and other social indices—amount of formal schooling, income, occupation, number of sources of public information regularly available—but were usually somewhat higher. That is, if it was found that college people as a group differed in particular opinions from people with less schooling, it was usually found that as a group the (relatively) well-informed people differed even more from the poorly informed people.

The Time Element

Public opinion of course reflects the period in which it is measured. As an issue unfolds—as it is debated more and more in the papers and on the radio—people who read about it or hear about it may undergo a change of feeling, and a trend poll may register some shift of opinion even within a short

period of time. The surveys that provide the main basis for
the contents of this book were made in the summer of 1946—
first in June, shortly before the Bikini tests of the atomic bomb,
and then again in August, shortly after those tests. There has
been much debate since then in world councils over the issue of
control of atomic energy. It might reasonably be expected,
therefore, that public opinion on this issue has changed. Unfortunately, no studies comparable to our 1946 surveys have
been made since then, although we have been able to draw upon
recent surveys on related matters for some of the interpretations in this book. But it may be pointed out that there is little
reason to believe that events during the last year have been such
as to cause any appreciable changes in the attitudes with which
we are most concerned. There is evidence that suspicion of
Russia declined somewhat and then rose again in the eight
months following August 1946, but it will become clear that
these changes would not have served to alter the conclusions
drawn from the surveys made at that time. The amount of
"publicity" required to alter markedly the general public's
interest in an issue—at least in the absence of an extremely
dramatic event that may suddenly and sharply illuminate its
importance—is enormous. The Baruch plan was publicly
announced when the interviewing for the June part of our
survey was well under way. Undoubtedly, it must have had
an effect upon people who were acutely conscious of the control
problem. But its effect upon the public as a whole, as judged
from our intensive survey interviews, was imperceptible.

In June 1946 it was found that 31 percent of the sample
were unable to give even the simplest answer to the question,
posed in the course of the intensive interview, "As you see it,
what is the main thing the United Nations organization is set
up to do?" In August, approximately the same proportion
(34 percent) were unable to answer the question. In April 1947

the question was posed again as part of another intensive survey by the Survey Research Center of the University of
Michigan; 33 percent were unable to make any reply to it. In
other words, it would appear that a third of the people live in
a world that psychologically does not include foreign affairs.
As for the other two-thirds, it must be said that at best, "despite
the tremendous network of newspapers, radio, magazines, and
other educational media, only a minority of the people can be
considered actively conversant with contemporary world
problems." Except perhaps among this minority, the development of new attitudes or new understanding appears to come
very slowly, or only as the result of extraordinary pressures.
It therefore appears to us safe to assume that the attitudes and
beliefs described in the succeeding chapters are still among
those that must be dealt with in appraising the role of the
people at this very early period of the Atomic Age.

CHAPTER II · PUBLIC AWARENESS
OF THE ATOMIC BOMB

THE KNOWLEDGE of the existence of the fabulous new instrument of destruction, the atomic bomb, has penetrated to even the most isolated members of the American adult population. Notwithstanding the fact that seven percent of the people in our intensive survey said they read no newspapers or magazines and had no radios, and an additional 13 percent reported only a limited access to these channels of news, at least 98 percent appeared to have heard of the atomic bomb. To the experienced investigator of public opinion and information, accustomed to discover very sizable proportions of the public who are unaware of most major events, this is a phenomenal finding.

It must at once be added, however, that among many Americans this knowledge does not go beyond the simple fact that their government has in its possession a powerful weapon called the atomic bomb. People's conceptions of it vary from the vaguest of notions to a sophisticated understanding of its nature or at least its significance. In the summer of 1946, only 30 percent were able to give any meaningful answer when asked to name the materials from which atomic energy is made, and only three percent knew and could recall the names uranium and plutonium. On the other hand, three-fourths of the adult population were aware, a few weeks before the first Bikini experiment, that the bomb was soon going to be tested somehow, and two-thirds were able to state that the targets would be ships. Shortly after the experiment, nine out of ten adults knew at least that some sort of test of the bomb had been made, and three out of four could state that the targets had been ships.

Unquestionably, the first announcement of the bomb made an extraordinary impact upon public awareness, and the highly publicized Bikini experiments had what may certainly be described as a tremendous audience. But it was at the time of these experiments, when publicity and interest were at a high point, that only three percent could name uranium and plutonium. Only eight percent could identify the name of General Leslie R. Groves as being associated in some way with atomic research. However unimportant it may be for the public to absorb such facts as these, that it did not do so in the circumstances suggests, at least, that interest in the experiments was perhaps merely an interest in a spectacular event.

But the level of public information about the bomb is of interest not for its own sake but for the light it may shed upon the extent of the people's concern about the bomb and their insights into the grave issues it has raised. In this connection, probably the two most important items of information about the bomb that the public should possess are: (1) that other countries than the United States have access to the means of discovering the "secret" of producing atomic energy, and (2) that scientists are agreed that there is little hope of discovering an effective military defense against atomic bombs.

The first point was raised in the poll by the following question: "As far as you know, is the secret of how to make atomic bombs known only by the United States, or do you think some other countries also know how to make atomic bombs?"

56% said they thought other countries already knew how to make the bombs.
30% said only the United States now knew the secret.
14% did not know.

Those who said that the United States alone had the secret, or who could not answer the question, were then asked, "How long do you think it will be before another country learns how to make atomic bombs?" Only seven percent of the sample named periods longer than five years, including two percent who mentioned periods of more than ten years or said that other countries would never learn the secret.

Even as regards the actual production of the bombs, few were willing to say that our monopoly would last long. In answer to the question (in the intensive survey), "How long do you think it will be before the other countries are able to make the atomic bomb?" a third would venture no predictions, but only two percent said "never," and only five percent said "a long time" or named periods as long as ten years. The rest indicated that they thought "it would not be long," and almost a quarter even went so far as to say, although somewhat tentatively, that some other country might already be in a position to produce the bombs.[9]

It is notable that the people who gave evidence of being poorly informed about world events differed only a little on these questions from the well-informed. As is generally the case, the "don't-know" answers came preponderantly from the poorly informed, but among those who expressed opinions —whatever their apparent level of information about world news—there was remarkable agreement on the opinion that the United States' monopoly of the knowledge of how to make atomic bombs would be at best short-lived.

No doubt, the wide acceptance of the view that the secret will not keep has been promoted not only by the public statements of experts but by the evidence of World War II that the United States has no monopoly on scientific genius. One caution must be inserted here, however. People can voice acceptance of a fact without incorporating it into their thinking —that is, without bringing it to bear upon their opinions. We

[9] Tables summarized in the text are given in detail in Appendix B.

shall consider later whether this acknowledgment of the accessibility to other nations of the bomb "secret" is as influential in the minds of the people as the knowledge that the United States can make atomic bombs and that so far no other country has given public evidence that it can do so.

Regarding the prospects for developing a defense against atomic bombs, the public was clearly not well-acquainted with expert opinion. In the intensive survey, the question was asked, "Do you think we will be able to work out a defense against the bomb before other countries learn how to make it?"

42% of the people thought we would do so.
26% thought we could not develop a defense.
32% were undecided, or could offer no opinions.

In the extensive survey, the question was slightly different: "Do you think the United States will be able to work out an effective defense against the atomic bomb before other nations could use it against us?"

55% said yes.
19% said no.
26% could offer no opinions.[10]

The marked prevalence of the opinion that we should be able to defend ourselves against atomic bombs if necessary (in spite of public statements to the contrary by leading scientists) suggests that there has been inadequate treatment of the question in the sources of public information. Even among people who appeared to be relatively well-informed about world affairs, the opinion that the United States would develop a defense by the time it might be needed was very widespread, although less so than among the poorly informed.

[10] The difference between the distributions of answers in the two surveys is probably due not only to differences in the wording of the questions but also to differences in the methods of recording responses and to sampling variation.

But the fact that people appeared to have a better understanding of the temporariness of our monopoly than they had of the prospects for finding a defense is probably not to be explained solely by possible differences in the publicity these two questions received. Both views may stem simply from faith in the inexhaustibility of scientific invention. The statements with which people explained their opinion that we should have a defense in time are illuminating: "Since the scientists were able to invent the bomb, they can work out a defense." "Our scientists are already working on a defense." "Every weapon produces a defense." Some expressed faith in the superiority of American genius and resources: "The United States will be able to keep ahead." "Our scientists made the bomb first; they can figure out a defense before the rest of the world catches up."

The people unquestionably have immense respect for the power of the bomb. Our intensive survey was made by means of hour-long interviews, in which each respondent was encouraged to express his ideas about the bomb and related subjects with the spontaneity of ordinary conversation. Not one percent of this representative sample of American adults depreciated the power of the bomb during these talks, or expressed the view that its potency had been exaggerated. While a plurality of those interviewed after Bikini expressed the opinion that the destruction there had been less than they had thought the bomb capable of, there was clear evidence that the people's respect for the power of the bomb had not been diminished by what many took to be its partial failure at Bikini. But it is highly questionable that this respect is anything more than a recognition that the bomb is the mightiest weapon yet produced by scientists who seem capable of producing novel weapons indefinitely, each more terrible than the last. There is little indication that the people recognize the revolutionary significance of the new weapon. The magnitude of the destruction it can wreak they have recognized, but its inescapability has not yet been borne in upon most of them.

One may, of course, interpret these attitudes as indications of an invincible faith in the power of the human mind to master any problem that confronts it. It is probably more realistic to make the interpretation that although the public is convinced that the bomb is a weapon of almost unbelievable destructiveness, it does not realize the implications of its existence for the world community. While it is clear that a large majority are aware of the bomb as a spectacular instrument of destruction, there is no evidence that this knowledge has served to intensify concern with our international relations. At any rate, the level of information about the international problem is very low. Roughly, it may be mentioned again that in surveys made in June and August 1946 and April 1947, one-third of the people were unable to say what the United Nations was designed to accomplish, in even such general terms as "to work for peace," "to get the countries of the world to cooperate." These people are probably scarcely aware, if not totally unaware, of the existence of the organization to which it has been proposed that the control of the bomb be entrusted. And it is to be noted that included in their number were one-fifth of the people who in the 1944 national election exercised their right to vote. A survey of a sample of the Iowa population conducted by the Iowa Poll (affiliated with the Des Moines *Register* and *Tribune*) shortly after the public release of the Baruch report indicated that only 39 percent in that state had heard or read anything about the report. In our own poll, taken at a time when the Secretary of State was very much in the international news, 57 percent of the people—including 48 percent of those who had voted in the previous national election—could not give his name.

Many other signs will appear, in the findings to be presented in the remaining chapters, that the people are not informing themselves to an extent that would indicate active concern about how the international problem is to be solved. The fact remains, however, that they know that the atomic bomb is terrible and is to be feared. The reasons why they do not show greater concern about its future must be sought elsewhere than in their attitudes toward its destructive power.

CHAPTER III · ARE THE PEOPLE CONCERNED?

EVIDENCES THAT THE PEOPLE are not deeply concerned about the atomic bomb problem are made doubly perplexing by the pessimism they display regarding the prospects for averting another world war. Polls by the National Opinion Research Center, Gallup, and other organizations indicate that since the first few months after the end of the war there has been an increase in the belief that there will be another war within twenty-five or even ten years. In the summer of 1946, according to these polls, about two-thirds of the people said they expected another war, involving the United States, within twenty-five years, and half these people predicted that it would come within ten years. Such findings as these cannot be taken as evidences of genuine concern, but they are certainly symptomatic of widespread pessimism. Results from our own poll question confirm the conclusion that the public was on the whole decidedly pessimistic at that time. Confronted with the question, "Which of these statements comes closest to your own ideas?" and the following four alternative answers, almost half the people rejected the opportunity to choose even a temperately optimistic statement of the prospects for averting war:

25% chose "I think there is bound to be another world war within the next twenty-five years."
23% chose "Things certainly are bad now, and it looks as though they will get worse, so there may be another world war within twenty-five years."

37% chose "Things don't look too good now, but the nations will work out ways of getting along better, so there may not be another world war within 25 years."

11% chose "I do not think there will be another world war within twenty-five years."

4% could not choose among these statements.[11]

The twenty-five percent who chose the most pessimistic answer came preponderantly from the least well-informed segment of the population—people who gave evidence of having little or no acquaintance with news of international significance. It is quite clear that among such people the belief that another war is certain springs from general pessimism about the ways of the world rather than from an appraisal of actual events. They support their predictions by such arguments as that "there always has been war, and there always will be," or else by expressions of a basic suspicion and hostility toward foreign nations and foreign ways. It is notable that whereas on most questions involving the atomic bomb from 25 to 40 percent of those characterized as poorly informed would venture no opinions, all but about 10 percent of such people expressed opinions in our poll regarding the prospects for war, and a third of them chose the most pessimistic statement.

Among better informed people, the statement most commonly chosen was one of qualified optimism: "The nations will work out ways of getting along better, so that there may not be another world war within twenty-five years." Undoubtedly many chose this statement out of hope, or out of loyalty to an idea, rather than because of conviction. The idea

[11] A poll reported by *Fortune* in July 1946 put the question this way: "Do you think that there will probably be another big war during the next 25 or 30 years, or do you think there is a fairly good chance to avoid it?" Forty-one percent said that there would be a "big war," 49.6 percent that there was "a good chance to avoid it," 9.4 percent didn't know.

of international cooperation and international organization as a means of preventing war has taken a strong hold in the minds of the people who think much about international relations, and they are reluctant to discount its possibilities. "Sitting down and talking things over," "getting together and ironing out differences," compromising, and arbitrating appeal to Americans as ethical and reasonable ideas, and in addition no other course of action suggests itself so obviously for the avoidance of war. But in the process of international "talking things over" international disagreements are inevitably widely publicized, usually as evidences of a lack of cooperativeness and of unethical motives on the other fellow's part, and there is reason to ask whether the people's faith is sturdy enough to withstand these strains. Shifts in public opinion not only about the prospects of war, but also, for example, about the desirability of world organization appear to follow closely upon changes in the general tone of the international news, particularly with respect to Russia's behavior in United States-Russian conferences and in the UN.

What part does the atomic bomb play in people's thinking about war? Two-thirds of the sample in the polling survey said "yes" to the question, "Do you think there is real danger that atomic bombs will ever be used against the United States?" Only about 25 percent were willing to take the position that there was no danger of atomic bombing of the United States. Moreover, half those who acknowledged the possibility that the United States might be attacked said there was at least a fair degree of danger that members of their own families might be killed in atomic bomb attacks. The small proportion who took a strongly optimistic view of the prospects for avoiding war for at least 25 years were somewhat less likely than the others to foresee a danger of atomic bombing of the United States, but even among them the predominant opinion was that the danger existed. On the other hand, people who asserted with great positiveness that we will be at war within that period were neither more nor less likely to say yes to the question about atomic bombings of the United States than those who tempered their predictions. A third of those who felt war is bound to come said either that the United States would never be subjected to atomic bomb attacks or else that they had no opinion on that question. Many poorly informed people, who tend to be most pessimistic about averting war, have no opinions on questions about the bomb. It might be expected that their pessimism would extend to the threat of atomic bombing also, for they have heard of the bomb, but apparently they give it little thought. Some whose pessimism about the duration of peace is based on a stereotyped suspicion of foreign countries have also a stereotyped opinion that foreign countries cannot equal our achievements and hence that they could not attack us with atomic bombs. Most people, however, even if they are hopeful that "the nations will work out ways of getting along," concede that the atomic bomb is a potential threat to us.

But there is a decided difference between acknowledging a dangerous possibility when attention is called to it and being acutely conscious of that possibility. The view that we might be attacked by atomic bombs is consistent with the view, accepted by the majority of the people, that we have no sure monopoly on the means of making the bombs. But that the danger may nevertheless appear simply hypothetical is suggested by the fact that our present exclusive possession of atomic bombs is ascendant in most people's minds over their acceptance of the judgment that this advantage is a temporary one. If the people were as apprehensive about the bomb as their recognition of its power and their pessimism about averting war may suggest, it is reasonable to suppose that the subject of the bomb would spring to the fore whenever they consider broad aspects of our international relations. But in intensive interviews about the UN and about the role of the United States in the world, the majority of people make no reference to the bomb unless the interviewer specifically directs their attention toward it. In the first half of our intensive interview in August 1946, in which interviewers employed twenty-five open questions dealing with the UN, our international relations generally, and our relations with Russia in particular, but not alluding to the bomb, only one person out of six brought up that subject spontaneously.[12] These references were mainly to the desirability of our keeping the bomb secret, or to Russia's presumed envy or fear of our possession of atomic bombs. People who think at all specifically about our international relations think about Russia. "Foreign affairs" was almost synonymous with Russia in the interviews just referred to; half the people mentioned Russia before the interviewers did so. In the poll, in answers to direct questions, two-thirds of the people named Russia as the foreign country most likely to know or to learn soon how to make atomic bombs. But whereas it appears to be the case that when

[12] Some of the questions were: "How satisfied are you with the way the United States has been getting along with other countries since the war ended? (Why?)" "Do you think the United States has made any mistakes in dealing with other countries since the end of the war? (What?)" "What do you think is the best thing that the United States could do to help keep peace in the world? (Why?)" "How about Russia—do you think the Russian Government is trying to cooperate with the rest of the world as much as it can? (Why?)" "Do you think we can count on the Russian Government to be friendly with us? (Why?)" "How do you feel about the general idea of having an organization like the UN? (Why?)" "How successful do you think the UN will be in keeping peace among the countries? (Why?)" "How would you feel about this country belonging to a world organization where we would have to follow the decisions of the majority of the nations? (Why?)" "Do you think this world organization should have armed forces to carry out its decisions if necessary? (Why?)"

people think "war" their thoughts then move to "Russia," it does not appear to be the case that they move necessarily to "atomic bomb."

Undoubtedly if there were actual apprehension rather than simply pessimism about war, the atomic bomb would be a far livelier topic in people's thinking. The people are intellectually aware that the bomb is a possible threat, but the threat is not strongly felt. Their own explanations of why they do not "worry" about the bomb make this clear. When the interviewers asked, "How worried are you about the atomic bomb?" only a quarter would admit to a state of personal concern. Half the respondents said they were not at all worried, others that they were worried very little. The relatively few who held consistently optimistic views about the bomb, indicating that they did not believe it to be a threat to us, were of course included among the "nonworriers." But most of the nonworriers acknowledged that the bomb represents a potential threat to our peace and security. The reasons they gave for not worrying were just such as they might give for not thinking much about any other social issue that does not compel their attention—that there is no use worrying about something you cannot do anything about, that such problems are problems for the government, for experts, not for the ordinary citizen. These quotations from interviews illustrate the variety of ways in which people indicated that the problem was not theirs to be concerned about; well-informed people were just as prone as poorly informed, voters as non-voters, to disclaim this responsibility:

> "I'm not worried about it. What's the use of worrying? If I did, there are other weapons that are worse being developed all the time, and I'd no sooner get over worrying about it than a worse one would come along. So what's the use?"

"Well, I think it's a terrible thing. I think they shouldn't kill people with it, and I think that I don't like it. But I'm not worried. It wouldn't do me any good."

"I don't think I devote much time to worrying about it. The building business is too complicated now for me to worry about the bomb. It's too remote."

"No, I don't care. I got everything I need. From the morning when I get up, I pick apples and I get a dollar a bushel. So why should I worry about that bomb? I don't need to worry. Let it come. I don't think about it."

"I'm not worried. It would be worse in those populated places. Lord knows this isn't a place where they would use it."

"I'm not worried. You can't be killed any deader by an atomic bomb than by a bullet or a blockbuster or anything else."

"Well, I just think it should be controlled. I'm just hoping that this suggestion made by the United States will bear fruit, because I feel if it isn't controlled we might as well decide we're going to the next world. I don't worry about it. I'm not that kind. If it comes, it comes, but I think if anything can be done about it . . ."

"I'm not worried. I think that the head officials or whatever it is would know how to use it."

"I feel like our government will take care of its own, and there is no need for me to worry about something I have no control over."

"No, I'm just like the rest. I know the bomb can wipe out cities, but I let the government worry about it."

"I let the people who are qualified in those things do the worrying. I am just one of the many people who accept circumstances as they are. To me, it is just like if you were living in a country where there were earthquakes. What good would it do you to go to bed every night worrying whether there would be an earthquake?"

It may be argued that in the face of a danger that is real, imminent, people are likely to worry *because* they feel they can do nothing to avert it. Hence these disclaimers may be construed as an indication that the bomb danger has little reality even in the minds of those who appear to be aware of it.[13] But what is perhaps more significant in these remarks, particularly because they are as characteristic of informed people as of uninformed people, is the attitude they reveal toward the citizen's role in our democracy. The belief that all a person can do is "let the government worry" extends to the threat of war, as well. The majority of the people believe that there is nothing they can do to help prevent war. Except in extreme emergencies, our government functions with few direct calls upon the people's attention. It is not surprising, then, that most people have little conception of how they participate or might participate in governmental policy-making, except for choosing at long intervals among candidates for elective offices. Accordingly there is a great psychological distance between the people and the world issues that concern their government.

[13] It may be argued, of course, that there is much more anxiety than people admit, but that it is repressed. A much more intensive probing would be required to demonstrate whether or not this is so.

CHAPTER IV · THE PEOPLE'S VIEWS ON INTERNATIONAL CONTROL OF ATOMIC ENERGY

THAT PEOPLE were not generally aware of how their leaders were dealing with the bomb problem even at a time when, with the Bikini experiment and the Baruch announcement, it was very much in the news is indicated by their reactions to questions about international control. One of these questions in our extensive survey was a specific one regarding the proposal to turn control of our atomic secrets over to the United Nations. The next was a general question about whether international control would be a good thing. The responses to the latter were as follows:

> "Which of these three statements comes closest to what you think the United States should do?"
> 22% chose "The United States should go on making atomic bombs, and not depend on systems of international control of the bomb."
> 47% chose "We should go on making atomic bombs for the time being, but try to work out a system of international control to prevent any nation, including our own, from using atomic bombs."
> 26% chose "We should stop making atomic bombs right now and try to work out a system of international control to keep other nations from making them too."
> 5% made no choice.

To the desirability of a system designed to prevent the use of atomic bombs, three-quarters of the people gave assent.

But when the issue was presented in specific terms embodying the most striking feature of the Baruch plan, the reactions were utterly different: The question, "Do you think the secret of making atomic bombs should be put under the control of the United Nations organization, or should the United States keep the secret to itself?" drew the following responses (the figures here are for August 1946; the June figures are almost identical):

18%: The secret should be put under UN control.
75%: The United States should retain the secret.
7%: Qualified answers or no opinion.

The more informed people appeared to be about world affairs, the more likely they were to approve of relinquishing control of the secret, but even among the eight percent at the top of the informational scale, this opinion was in the minority.

Judging from the way in which they discussed this issue in the intensive survey, it seems clear that most people identified neither question with the Lilienthal report or with the Baruch proposal that had been announced a short time before. The reaction to the first question was the reaction characteristically elicited by any proposal, couched in general terms, for preventing war. That the second question represented a measure that the United States had proposed for the promotion of that objective was apparent to only a very small proportion of respondents. It was taken by most people to mean "giving away" the secret, a foolhardy jeopardizing of our own security, a rash distribution of a weapon that ought surely to be kept under lock and key. In the intensive survey the question was asked only of people (two-thirds of the sample) who gave some indication of understanding what the UN is; an overwhelming majority wanted the secret kept in the United States. Three in ten of these gave as their reason that if we did not keep it "other countries will use the bomb." About the same number pointed out that "the bomb is in good hands here." Two in ten argued that to give up the secrets would be foolish because they constituted a "protection" for us, that as long as we have the secret "other countries are afraid of us." One in ten said that we had a "right" to keep it because we had developed the bomb, that it was "ours." Fewer than two out of ten of those who opposed the UN-control idea offered arguments based on defects of the proposal *as a means of achieving control*, such as that "other countries might get the secret from the UN," or that "the UN is not strong enough to exercise control." It was not clear that even the small group who approved of the proposal understood that it was designed as a practical measure for our own protection as well as that of the rest of the world. Many of them said only that "we might as well give the secret to them because they'll find it out anyway," or that such a step would show our faith in UN and make other countries less fearful and envious of us.

Our "secrets" question undoubtedly posed the control issue in its most "unfavorable" light, in view of people's unfamiliarity with its background. If the question had been preceded in the interview by some explanation of the objectives of the proposal and of the safeguards with which our present advantages were to be protected, it might have been accorded a less unfavorable reception. An attempt to present the question in that way was made after the Baruch announcement by the Iowa Poll with a sample of the population of that state: "Our government is willing to swap the atomic bomb for world peace. After the nations get together on a complete plan to control atomic energy: (A) The United States will stop making atomic bombs. (B) The United States will destroy the ones we have. (C) The United States will turn over to the United Nations authority our 'know-how' on atomic energy.

Does this sound good or bad to you?" Forty percent said it sounded good, 50 percent that it sounded bad, 10 percent were undecided. (It should be noted that the magical term "secrets" was not employed in the question.) Even in the reasoned context provided in the Iowa question, only 40 percent of Iowans favored the plan. And taking public information as it actually stood, it is clear that our monopoly appeared much more valuable than the idea of UN control.

In May 1946 the National Opinion Research Center had asked a series of questions about control of the bomb, the responses to which indicated a generally favorable reaction to the idea of international action to prevent the use of atomic bombs—including the principle of inspection, which 75 percent said they favored. It is significant, however, that to the questions in the series which indicated the United States might have to give up some current advantage, the reaction was decidedly less favorable, and when it was suggested that inspection might cost us our monopoly of the bomb secret, almost half those who had previously expressed approval of international inspection retracted it.

Why, since people apparently were aware that our hold over the secrets will probably not last long, did they attach such importance to it? Part of the answer, certainly, is that our monopoly is the present reality; to take eventualities into account calls for a perspective that relatively few are able to bring to bear on international issues, which, even without such additional complexities, may be only dimly apprehended. This is not simply a matter of failing to put two and two together; it is also evident that the two factors—*a*, what we are known to have, and, *b*, what it is said other countries will be able to attain in the future—represent very unequal quantities and are far from equally prominent in people's thinking. In the intensive survey, many people, even after they had said in answer to a direct question that other countries would find out how to make atomic bombs before long, continued to discuss other questions about the bomb wholly within the framework of our monopoly.

Moreover, the people's willingness to "try" international control is often unaccompanied by any conviction that it can be made to work. Whereas 73 percent of the people in our poll had indicated approval of having the United States "try to work out a system of international control" to prevent the use of atomic bombs, only 37 percent responded affirmatively to the question, "Do you think a system of international supervision and control can prevent all countries from making atomic bombs and using them against each other?" Even in the group who might be thought of as most receptive to the idea of international control—the 18 percent who favored our turning our bomb secrets over to UN control—only a little more than half thought international supervision and control could prevent atomic war. (Their reasons for approving UN control of the secrets, it will be recalled, were mainly that we could not keep the secrets anyway, and that turning them over to the UN would be an act of good will.) Consistently enough, among this 18 percent the opinion that "we should go on making atomic bombs for the time being" was just as prevalent as it was among those who opposed turning the secret over to UN control.

Of all those—irrespective of their views on UN control of the secrets—who said they favored discontinuing our bomb production and working toward international control, only four in every ten thought international supervision and control could prevent atomic war. Of those who favored making bombs temporarily but working toward international control, again four in ten thought international supervision and control could prevent atomic war. These data might be summarized in this way:

14% took an apparently consistent position against international control—that is, that we should continue to make atomic bombs without striving for international control, and that such control could not be effective anyway.

35% expressed approval of trying to work out a system of international control, but also the opinion that international supervision and control could not prevent atomic warfare. (Nineteen percent of these people approved turning the secrets over to UN control.)

31% took an apparently consistent position in favor of international control—that is, that we should strive toward such a system and that international supervision and control could be effective in preventing atomic warfare. (Thirty-two percent of this particular group favored turning the secrets over to UN control.)

20% were undecided or without opinions on either or both questions.

Thus, not only did our present monopoly weigh more heavily in people's thinking than the prospect that other countries may soon be able to produce atomic bombs; it seemed also to weigh more heavily than the putative benefits of a proposal which, however meritorious as a principle, depends upon the compliance, the honor, the good will of foreign countries.

More recently—in April 1947—the Survey Research Center of the University of Michigan conducted a national intensive survey in which a few questions regarding atomic energy control were asked of those people—again two-thirds of the sample—who gave evidence of understanding what the UN is. The first of these questions was, "In your opinion, should there be international control of atomic bombs, or should each country remain free to make its own bombs?" About 40 percent of those asked said there should be international control; an equal proportion said each country should be free to make atomic bombs; the remainder gave qualified or uncertain answers or had no opinions. If the question had been asked of the entire sample—including the most poorly informed one-third—the results would probably have been less favorable to international control, for the less well-informed among those who were asked were appreciably less receptive to the idea of international control than those higher up on an informational scale.

Now here was a question that might have been expected to elicit rather strong support for international control, because the alternative was baldly presented as having "each country remain free to make its own bombs," a reminder to respondents of the fact that other countries might soon discover atomic energy for themselves. Yet half the respondents with opinions on the subject rejected the idea of international control, even when presented in that light. By April 1947 international control had evidently become somewhat more identified in people's minds with giving up our atomic secrets; although no reference to "secrets" was made in the question, one of the two most frequently given reasons for opposing international control was that the secrets are ours, we have a right to keep them. The other reason was that other countries cannot be trusted, that international control would not work.

Among those who favored international control as against the alternative indicated by the question, the reasoning was that "it's the only way to try to prevent atomic war." [14] Asked then, "Do you think it is possible to set up an international control system which would prevent atomic war?" less than

[14] It is of interest that only a few people, either in April 1947 or in June or August 1946, mentioned as one of their reasons for supporting international control that it would speed the development of constructive uses of atomic energy. The number of such references would of course have been larger if the surveys had been oriented around the general topic of atomic energy rather than the bomb. But it was the opinion of the analysts, based on experimental interviews before the 1946 surveys were under way, that public awareness of atomic energy apart from the bomb was negligible. According to those who worked on the experimental interviews, "To the general public atomic energy means the atomic bomb."

one-third of those who preferred international control gave an unqualified "yes." Only about a fifth said flatly "no," but the "yesses" of the remainder were qualified or uncertain. The qualifications were "if the countries would cooperate," "it's a good idea, but Russia won't go along." These qualifications are eminently sensible, but they raise some further questions about the sturdiness of such approval of international control as we do find in surveys. People appear to be readily receptive to the idea that—unlike the United States—other countries do not cooperate, and there is little in the headlines these days to undermine such skepticism. As we shall see later, their conception of the workings of our foreign policy tends to be that the United States tries its best to cooperate, whereas other countries are willful, selfish, unreasonably demanding. When people volunteered criticism of our government's policies abroad, it was usually that our government had been too generous, too yielding, more conciliatory than fairness requires. People are usually willing to assent to any proposal for United States "cooperation" with other countries if it is couched in broad enough terms. But when our contributions to international cooperation are specifically defined, they are more likely than not to be seen as endangering, or at least not advancing, our own security and well-being.

Moreover, international cooperation is not the only principle that has emerged from the war. Considerable evidence can be adduced from surveys that the need for maintaining strong armed forces is also an idea to which there is ready agreement. Considering how concrete and easily understandable the latter idea is, it may be well to examine further what our participation in international cooperation means to people who accept it as a general principle.

CHAPTER V · THE PEOPLE'S UNDERSTANDING OF THE ROLE OF THE UNITED STATES IN THE WORLD

THE REACTION to the three choices offered in our poll regarding what the United States should do about the atomic bomb (page 30) is representative of people's reactions to any broad proposition that obviously demands either accepting or rejecting the principle of international cooperation for the promotion of peace. When the following proposition was presented in our intensive survey: "Some people would like to see our government keep to itself and not have anything to do with the rest of the world. How would you feel about that?" three-quarters of the people rejected the idea of isolation, most of them emphatically, and only 15 percent, mainly among the least informed, found it acceptable:

> "I don't think we should do that. I don't think we would get along very well that way. We have to cooperate with all of them. If we sat out here to ourselves, soon there wouldn't be any sale for our stuff. We can't isolate ourselves from our neighbors here in town, and the same is true with countries."

> "It can't be done. No good feeling would be created by that. It's just like leaving your neighbor alone—you can't be friendly that way."

> "No, it would be very wrong. Our country can't get along in the world by itself. For instance, if Hitler had conquered the whole of Europe, we couldn't have stood alone. So we can't keep to ourselves today."

"No, definitely. We can't be isolationists. Whatever happens to one nation is bound to have its effect on all the others. We're too close to each other in this age of airplanes and atomic bombs."

"That would be fine if we could do it, but it seems like we can't any more. [Why not?] Well, we have to help settle the peace treaties and everything. How can we keep to ourselves?"

"I'm afraid that day's over. The world is too small nowadays. I don't think we could or should."

"Well, I don't think we can hardly do that. With the radio and airplanes—things are so developed. Radio broadcasts bring us the news almost immediately. There is such a change in our way of living, and we need things from other countries—like bananas—and they need things from us."

Many people referred, at least incidentally, to the necessity of trading with other countries, but, even so, isolation as a policy was rejected not primarily for economic reasons but on more general grounds. "The world is too small" to permit such a policy. The analogy with "our town," "our neighbors," was made again and again. We have to get along with people living around us; the nation has to get along with other nations.

An organization designed to facilitate this getting along is obviously a good thing. When those who were familiar with the United Nations were asked, "How do you feel about the general idea of having an organization like the United Nations?" two-thirds expressed unqualified approval, a quarter expressed qualified or simply unenthusiastic approval, and only five percent disapproved. Approval was expressed usually as a general endorsement of all efforts to preserve peace:

"I think it's a fine idea. They are trying to pick out the best ways to bring peace among all nations."

"The idea is fine. I'm all for it. I'd like to see wars abolished from the face of the earth, and that's what the UN will stand for."

"It's a good idea. Anything that can bring about a compromise of disputes short of going to war is worth any effort to make it work."

Such a notion as a federation of nations under a central government seemed to most people—the relatively well-informed as well as the poorly informed—to be extreme and unworkable:

"Do you think it would be possible to organize the nations of the world in the same way the states in this country are organized, with a government over them all to make laws that they would have to obey?"

	June 1946	August 1946
Yes, or yes with qualifications	26%	25%
Undecided, don't know	12	11
No, or no with qualifications	62	64

But the suggestion that the United States should participate in an organization "where we would have to follow the decisions of the majority of the nations" found greater favor, particularly among those who were sufficiently well informed about world affairs to have some acquaintance with the objectives of the United Nations. The fact that this proposal was in less favor in August than in June was perhaps a reflection of the growth of dissatisfaction with Russia's behavior that took place at the same time.

"How would you feel about this country belonging to a world organization where we would have to follow the decisions of the majority of the nations?" [15]

[15] In our interviews, this question followed immediately after the one about the feasibility of a federation of nations. Probably some were influenced in their reactions to the second question by the phrasing of the first one.

	All respondents		Those acquainted with UN	
	JUNE	AUG.	JUNE	AUG.
Approve, or approve with qualifications	44%	36%	53%	47%
Undecided, don't know	14	12	9	7
Disapprove, or disapprove with qualifications	42	52	38	46

Some polls have shown even greater support for a world organization of extensive powers. The issue is obviously un-crystallized, at least so far as public familiarity with it is concerned, and the reactions found in surveys are heavily dependent upon how the questions are phrased. Elmo Roper reported in the summer of 1946 [16] that 63 percent of the population responded affirmatively to the following question: "If every other country in the world would elect representatives to a world congress, with a strict provision that all countries have to abide by the decisions, whether they like them or not, would you be willing to have the United States go along on this?" The Gallup Poll reported, August 18, 1946, that 54 percent approved and only 24 percent disapproved of the suggestion that "the United Nations organization should be strengthened to make it a world government with power to control the armed forces of all nations, including the United States." The National Opinion Research Center, summarizing the results of a number of such polls in its publication *Opinion News*, April 15, 1947, points out that there are "many indications that the people of the United States are, by and large, coming to reject isolationism as a primary element of American foreign policy." More boldly in the same connection, *Fortune*, in March 1947, declares that "proof that isolation is a dead duck" has become "superfluous."

But it is of critical significance that the people's responsive-

[16] In his column in the *New York Herald-Tribune*, August 1, 1946.

ness to the principle of international cooperation diminishes sharply whenever it is tested against a more or less concrete example of how such a principle would be applied. It is notable, for example, that whereas 63 percent responded favorably to Roper's question about the United States "going along" on a plan for a world congress (the question quoted above), in the same poll only 47 percent responded favorably to the following question: "If every other country in the world would turn over to a world organization all their military secrets, and allow continuous inspection, would you be willing for the United States to go along with this?" In a *Fortune* survey published in March 1947, whereas 71 percent were found to consider maintaining our military forces "at about their present strength" more important than balancing the national budget, only 56 percent considered "continuing to send food to needy countries" more important than balancing the budget, and only 14 percent chose "continuing making loans to foreign nations" rather than balancing the budget.[17]

It is evident from these figures that the friendly reactions to proposals for international cooperation do not indicate, as it has been suggested that they do, "the degree to which the people of this country have accepted the facts and the necessity of international cooperation as a fundamental United States responsibility." "International cooperation" makes its appeal to the desire for peace. "Sending food to needy countries" makes its appeal to humanitarian impulses. But "making loans to foreign nations" apparently must make its appeal to an understanding of practical aspects of international cooperation, and that appeal fails.

Most of the people do not see what it is the United States gains by extending credits to foreign countries. Their reasoning about a loan abroad is based—if they are favorable to it—

[17] The polls mentioned here are shown in more detail in Appendix B.

on friendliness to the borrowing country and a belief in its neediness, or—if they are unfavorable toward it—mainly on the feeling that we cannot afford to keep giving money away. Loans are seen as an imposition on our economy, involving sacrifices for which there will be no material compensation. Asked point-blank in a survey whether they think the economic well-being of other countries makes any difference to our own, most of the people say that it does. Asked whether the encouragement of world trade is a good thing, most people say it is. Asked whether we have to buy from abroad in order to sell abroad, most people say we do. But these are not the terms in which they were thinking, obviously, when they answered the *Fortune* question about making loans rather than balancing the budget, and for the most part these are not the terms in which they considered the British loan, which, according to surveys conducted when the loan issue was before Congress, was opposed by more people than favored it.

In our intensive survey in August 1946, 50 percent of the people, when told that Congress had recently voted to "lend a large amount of money to England," said they thought the loan should not have been made. Most of these stated their opinions without any qualifications. Only 37 percent approved, half this number with qualifications or uncertainty. [18] The reasoning of those who disapproved was that the British already owed us too much, that the loans would not be repaid, that we could not afford to make such loans. Even among the

[18] In our June survey, before Congress approved the loan, a similar question produced a very similar distribution of opinions. Some polls asked the question only of people who said they had heard or read about the loan; among such people a larger minority—but still a minority—approved of the loan. The proposal to "lend a large amount of money to Russia" drew even less support. In June, 29 percent indicated approval, usually qualified; 58 percent disapproval, usually unqualified. In August, when general feelings toward Russia had grown more unfavorable, only 22 percent gave even qualified approval; 65 percent disapproved.

small group (18 percent) who favored the loan unqualifiedly, only one-third referred to possible beneficial effects upon our trade or the world economic situation; most of them argued simply that England needed our help. Those who gave qualified approval made the qualifications that we should lend the money only if England really needed it, or if we could make sure that it would be repaid. Even when asked directly, "Do you think we have anything to gain from making the loan?" 40 percent said no, an additional 15 percent that they did not know. Many named "England's friendship" as a gain, although most of these people believed that we could count on England's friendship in any case, and named it as a "gain" because apparently they could think of no other. Only 14 percent volunteered the answer that the loan might benefit us through its effect on American trade or business or on world trade in general.

The similarity between these reactions and the reactions toward turning control of the atomic bomb over to an international agency is that in both cases people appeared unaware that these programs were intended to have concrete benefits for us, as well as for others. They were seen as programs of giving to others, doing for others, not for ourselves. Some programs of this kind are approved, or at least countenanced, out of a humanitarian or friendly spirit. But it is doubtful that generosity alone could serve as a stable basis for public opinion on foreign economic policy. It can scarcely serve as any basis at all for decisions involving the atomic bomb. Jerome Bruner, in his study of wartime opinion called *Mandate from the People*,[19] declared that "our greatest long-term danger is the failure of Americans to understand their self-interest in international collaboration. Public support for international issues

[19] Duell, Sloan and Pearce, New York, 1944.

stands or falls with our conceptions of the *quid pro quo*." The second sentence, at least, seems incontrovertible.

The people have apparently come to understand that the oceans no longer insulate us against frequent contact with other countries. They hope we can work out ways of getting along amicably, and they recognize that some sort of world community organization—UN, world congress, an international police force—may be important in achieving international stability. But they have not yet seen clearly the concrete and specific actions that are implicit in the general principles they endorse.

Our Moral Superiority

In the main, people felt dissatisfied with the state of world affairs in 1946. Asked in our intensive survey, "Now that the war is over, how do you feel about the way the countries of the world are getting along these days?" seven out of ten expressed themselves as dissatisfied. When asked what they thought of "the way the UN has worked out so far"—even though most of them had just expressed strong approval of "the idea of having such an organization"—half thought UN was functioning unsatisfactorily, and most of the more favorable verdicts were qualified or unenthusiastic. The nations are "bickering and squabbling." They "don't seem to be getting anywhere."

Their own country, on the other hand, seemed to them to be trying steadfastly to achieve justice and harmony. It was, if anything, too generous with its material goods, and too lenient toward those governments which place obstacles in the road toward these goals. Thus, although only 15 percent said they were satisfied with "the way the countries of the world are getting along," almost two-thirds expressed themselves as at least fairly well-satisfied with the way the United States was behaving toward other countries. They felt that "we are making every effort," "doing the best we can." Among the 26 percent who expressed dissatisfaction with our own behavior toward other countries, the main criticisms were that we had been sending too much material aid abroad, and that we had been too lenient in our policies:

> "I don't think we're tough enough, to tell you the truth. You can call any American a sucker."

> "We are too soft. With Russia our attitude has been more appeasement than anything else. We should have taken a different stand in the beginning."

> "I feel the United States has been more than lenient. She has tried to see everybody's point of view, has tried to work things out, and hasn't walked out [of the UN]. I feel other nations are not cooperating as they should, and they have more to gain than we have. It was organized for them, not us."

> "I just think we have been pretty lenient with all of them. We are consistently handing out money and food to them and depriving ourselves. There is no use in that. . . . I believe in helping out, but they shouldn't strip us down."

Asked directly, "Do you think the United States has made any mistakes in dealing with other countries since the end of the war?" although only 30 percent (mainly among those least informed about world affairs) were willing to say that we had made no mistakes, more than half were unable to think of any such mistakes. The only criticisms of any prominence were that we had not been firm enough (especially toward Russia— a view then receiving prominent official sanction within the government) and that we were sending too much material aid abroad.

The basic attitudes involved here are neatly summarized in

two ingenious questions posed in a *Fortune* survey and reported in January 1947:

"Which of these statements do you think best describes what
the men who have been in charge of our relations with foreign
countries in the past ten years have been trying to do?"

"They have nearly always tried to help the rest of the world, even if what they did wasn't always the best thing for America."	19.7%
"They have tried to help the rest of the world and America at the same time, believing that what was the best thing for the world was the best thing for America."	34.8
"They have looked out for America first but at the same time have tried not to do anything that hurt the rest of the world too much."	24.7
"They have tried to look out for America first, last, and all the time, and have not cared too much what happened to the rest of the world."	4.4
Don't know.	16.4

"Which of these statements best describes what we should try
to do, now and in the future?"

"We must do the best we can for the rest of the world, even if what we do isn't always the best thing for America."	4.2%
"We must try to help the rest of the world and America at the same time, since what is best for the world is best for America."	32.5
"We must look out for America first, but at the same time we must try not to do anything that will hurt the rest of the world too much."	43.1
"We must look out for our own interests first, last and all the time, and not care too much about what happens to the rest of the world."	8.4
Don't know.	11.8

Few sanction "not caring about what happens to the rest of the world." But whereas only a minority are willing to grant that "what is best for the world" must necessarily be "what is best for America," the majority believe that their government has been guided by this or an even more generous ideal.

The people's belief in the generous motives of their own government stands in decided contrast to their skepticism regarding the motives that underlie the behavior of other countries. Even England, a country which most of the American people regard as our natural ally, is suspect. To the question, "Do you think the English Government is trying to cooperate with the rest of the world as much as it can?" four in every ten answered no, or no with qualifications; three in ten said yes, or yes with qualifications. The charge against England was that "she wants as much power as she can get," that she is imperialistic, that she cares only for her own interests. In explaining, in answer to another question, why they believe the United States "can count on the English Government to be friendly with us"—an opinion held by all but a small proportion of the people—it is notable that the argument that England *needs* us was at least as prominent as the argument that the two nations are bound together by traditional ties and a common language.

The people's view of Russia was extremely unfavorable. As of August 1946, only 25 percent believed that we could perhaps "count on the Russian Government to be friendly with us," on the grounds that Russia does not want war, or is afraid of us, or will find it profitable to stay on good terms with us. Responses to this question show a definite fluctuation in feeling from time to time, but the view that we can count on a friendly Russia remains steadily a minority one: In June 1946, 36 percent said yes to the question (or yes with qualifications); in August, 25 percent; in December, 39 percent. Although this form of the question has not been repeated in subsequent surveys, it is probably safe to say that the proportion of those answering yes would have dropped again in the summer of 1947. The question, "Do you think the Russian Government is trying to cooperate with the rest of the world as much as it can?" was asked in our intensive survey in June and August 1946, and in another survey of the same type in December. In each case an overwhelming majority answered no; there was a tendency to be less emphatic in this opinion in June and December than in August, but at no time were as many as 20 percent willing to say, even with qualifications, that Russia might be trying to cooperate. Scarcely two percent explained Russia's behavior as stemming from fear of other countries—from a desire to increase her security. People simply argued that Russia wants to increase her power and will do anything to that end, or just that Russia is arbitrary, self-willed, and generally untrustworthy.[20] National polls conducted by other agencies about the same time as our surveys found that from a quarter to a third of the public expressed the view that Russia was primarily interested in security rather than in imperialist expansion. But this opinion seemed to play almost no part in the spontaneous moral appraisals of Russia expressed in answer to open questions in our intensive surveys.

If people's failure to see the *quid pro quo* of international

---

[20] Interestingly enough, only a very small proportion explained their suspicions of Russia by the argument that she is trying to spread communism. Undoubtedly, if questioned directly about that argument, many would agree with it. But few spontaneously expressed such a view or argued that the Russian form of government makes discord with the United States or the rest of the world inevitable. People's feelings about Russia seem to be based far less on ideological grounds than on a general belief that she is indifferent to all values except self-interest. Roper, in a poll reported in his column in the *New York Herald Tribune* of October 17, 1946, found so many people unable to answer four elementary informational questions about the Russian system—involving freedom of the press, suffrage, individual enterprise, and freedom of religion—that he concluded the subject was "one of our largest national areas of ignorance."

cooperation stands in the way of their supporting it, their moral rating of foreign countries stands in the way of their believing cooperation is feasible. In our extensive survey people were asked:

"With which of these four statements do you come closest to agreeing?"

"It is very important to keep on friendly terms with Russia, and we should make every effort to do so."   13%

"It is important for the U.S. to be on friendly terms with Russia, but not so important that we should make too many concessions to her."   50

"If Russia wants to keep on friendly terms with us, we shouldn't discourage her, but there is no reason why we should make any special effort to be friendly."   17

"We shall be better off if we have just as little as possible to do with Russia."   16

No opinion.   4
                                                             ——
                                                            100%

Among those who chose the first statement—"we should make every effort" to keep on good terms with Russia—36 percent said in reply to another question that a system of international control and supervision of atomic energy production would not work. Among those who chose any of the other statements regarding our official position toward Russia, more than half said international control would not work. Among those who favored "making every effort," 32 percent favored putting "the secret of making atomic bombs" under UN control; in the groups choosing each of the other statements about policy toward Russia, that proposal was favored by 22, 12, and 7 percent respectively.

Among people who said in our intensive survey that we

could count on England's friendship, 43 percent said they would approve of U.S. participation in "a world organization where we would have to follow the decisions of the majority of the nations"; of those who said we could not count on England's friendship, only 30 percent approved of that idea. Similarly, half of those who thought we could count on Russia, but only a third of those who thought we could not, approved of the world organization idea.

It is understandable enough that people should be averse to entering into critical cooperative enterprises with partners whom they distrust. But it must not be overlooked that the contrast the people drew between their own government and other governments was based not on approval or disapproval of specific policies or actions, but on generalized "feelings." In spite of the fluctuations of opinion shown by trend questions about Russia—fluctuations that undoubtedly reflect the variations in the news of Russian behavior in international councils—intensive surveys show a very low level of awareness of just what it is that Russia and the others are differing about.

Moreover, the conception the people have of their own government as cooperative, "doing its best," seems to be an evidence, not of their approval of its postwar policies, but of a generally uncritical attitude. For example, on March 12, 1947, President Truman made the address in which he described his program of direct aid to Greece and Turkey. According to a Gallup release a month later, when asked, "Do you think the problem of aid to Greece and Turkey should be turned over to the United Nations organization?" 63 percent of a national sample said yes, only 23 percent no. But when, also in April, the following question was put in an intensive survey by the Survey Research Center to the two-thirds of a national sample who showed some familiarity with the UN: "Do you think the United States has been taking its problems to the UN as much as it should, or do you think we have been trying to work by ourselves too much?" 56 percent said we had worked through the UN enough, only 21 percent that we had not. In discussing the question, only a small proportion of those who had been questioned made specific reference to our program for Greece, either as an example of how we were not working with the UN, or as an example of a problem the UN could not deal with adequately.

Any question about whether the United States *should* support the United Nations, should strive to strengthen it, is likely to elicit majority approval. Even when feelings against Russia appeared to be most irritated, as in August 1946, most people unqualifiedly opposed the proposition in our intensive survey that "the United States ought to have more say in the UN than the other big countries," and unqualifiedly assented to the proposition that "if the United States and another country had a disagreement which they could not settle, the UN should have the power to tell both of them what ought to be done." But there is a marked tendency to take on faith the government's support of UN, and an issue that might have called this belief into question apparently received little attention.

But it has by now become apparent that international problems in general receive disappointingly little careful attention. We can elicit opinions in surveys by asking people direct questions, but on re-examination we find that many of these are not questions the people are asking themselves. As with the problem of what to do about the atomic bomb, the people are apparently letting the government do the worrying. And they appear to accept as a matter of course that, if the government errs, unlike other governments it will not err in the direction of too great self-interest.

CHAPTER VI · CONCLUSION

As THIS IS WRITTEN, it is more than a year and a half since Bernard Baruch announced the American proposals for world control of atomic energy. A headline in the special "Atomic Supplement" published August 1947 by the *Washington Post* summarizes its status: "As Pessimism Grows Over U.S.-Russian Collision, Alternatives Urged to End Control Impasse in U.N. Commission." The "alternatives urged," although differing from each other in critical ways, have in common the idea of establishing a far-reaching international organization—a federation of nations, a world government. Already the emphasis merely on yielding our atomic "secrets" to international control begins to appear narrow and insufficient to many who have led in espousing such a measure, although to most of the general public such a step still appears as a rash relinquishing of a valuable national safeguard.

This is not to say that the public would be more opposed to ideas of world organization than to the idea of turning our bomb secrets over to UN control. Indeed among those who appeared in August 1946 to understand what the UN is, fewer than two in ten approved of "turning the secret of the bomb over to the UN" rather than trying to keep the secret exclusively in the possession of the United States, but almost half of the same group felt at least somewhat favorable toward "having this country belong to a world organization where we would have to follow the decisions of the majority of the nations." But we have seen that a general proposition, couched in terms that appear fair, "democratic," and by definition directed toward the promotion of peace and harmony, invariably elicits greater approval than a specific proposal such as making loans, lowering tariff barriers, giving up control of our monopoly of the bomb. The people are not thinking practically and concretely in "one-world" terms. Their conception of cooperating internationally is largely negative; for many it means little more than "having no aggressive ambitions," "being friendly."

"On the level of generalities, the people seem friendly, cooperative, and even international in outlook. However, when specific issues are raised they are apt to deviate from this position. Frequently they fail to see the relation between specific action and the general values they have expressed. . . . While they tend strongly to apply the traditional American values of majority rule, equal rights, and fair play for the little fellow to general considerations of international affairs, they fall into many inconsistencies when specific problems are raised. . . . On the level of principle, most of the people who have some familiarity with the United Nations support the proposition that this country should have no greater voice in the UN than do the other large nations. They agree that the UN should have the power to settle disagreements involving the United States. Americans generally, however, are not often inclined to view world problems from the viewpoint of other nations as well as their own. . . . It seems clear that for many Americans the general principles of international cooperation which they are now willing to endorse will be placed under severe strain if specific developments in the United Nations seem to place the interests of the United States in a disadvantaged position." [21]

[21] Quoted from Part II of the report on *Public Reaction to the Atomic Bomb and World Affairs*, Cornell University, April 1947. Part II was prepared by Angus Campbell, Sylvia Eberhart, and Patricia Woodward.

Without far greater understanding of the reciprocal benefits of the specific contributions we are called upon to make to international cooperation, public approval of increasing world organization will be dubious at best. It is not remarkable that many should feel sentiments similar to those of the respondent quoted earlier who said, speaking of the UN, "They [other countries] have more to gain than we have." It is apparently never the United States that seeks help from abroad. We gave Lend-Lease. We make loans and gifts to needy countries and to countries like England (whose neediness is by no means apparent to the general public and who still, they point out, owes us money from the last war). We are asked to give up our bomb secrets, even though they are unquestionably in the best possible hands so long as we alone hold them. What is it *we* get?

The obvious implication here is that a far-reaching program of public education on our economic and political interdependence with the rest of the world is sorely needed. Jerome Bruner suggested that perhaps the way to modernize the people's 19th Century notions of tariff, for example, would be with such headlines as "Tariff Raises Grocery Bill Three Dollars a Week." [22] Our position as a creditor nation might become more than a measure of our generosity and our greater wealth and industry if foreign credits were translated concretely into jobs for workers, markets for farmers—something tangible and desirable for us.

Obviously such a suggestion is beset with difficulties, only one of which is the low level of public understanding of even relatively elementary economic phenomena. For example, the Treasury Department discovered through researches into public attitudes toward buying war bonds that most of the people could see no relation between bond-buying and keep-

[22] *Mandate from the People.* Duell, Sloan and Pearce, New York, 1944.

ing prices down, or between bond-buying and postwar employment levels, even when the existence of such a relation was suggested to them. In the people's minds, the government sold bonds to get money to buy war equipment, and the only patriotic reason for buying them was "to help the war effort" in that concrete way. It was agreed by officials that "over the long run a better understanding of the nature of the nation's economic problems would result in larger sales of bonds," but the pressure of time did not permit sacrificing short-run for long-run benefits. In the main, in spite of its reluctance to do so and its attempts to find a compromise solution, the Treasury had "to take public opinion where it stood" and make the best of it.[23]

It may be now that only the long-run view of educating people about their country's problems will serve. During the war it was possible for leaders to persuade people to "do the right thing" even if not for the right reasons; other reasons could serve; reasons against doing the right thing were not much of a force in people's thinking. An utterly different situation prevails now. The "right things to do" are very much at issue and innumerable arguments can be marshalled from people's prejudices and misunderstanding for not doing them.

What stands out in any detailed survey of public opinion is that much of the business that so deeply preoccupies their leaders goes on above people's heads. They appear either unaware of the issues confronting the government or uninformed about the reasons for the courses of action it adopts or proposes. Some of the people are physically as well as psychologically beyond the reach of news about the great issues of their time, as witness the reaction of a woman approached by an interviewer at 4:45 on a work day:

---

[23] From an unpublished manuscript by Dorwin Cartwright on the Treasury's wartime research.

"Now, listen here! I'm a working woman—work down there in the cotton mills every day now and have my home to take care of and these kids to look after. [The interviewer notes that she saw four children and heard another crying in another room.] We aren't on no mail route. We don't get no paper and we ain't got no radio. I wouldn't turn it on if we did—I don't like them. And so I don't know a thing about what you are asking about. I will try to answer your questions, but I am warning you, I don't know nothing about them other countries nor what this country ought to do with them."

But not many are so completely cut off from communication as this woman. Eighty-five percent of the people have radios, 80 percent say they read daily newspapers, more than half read magazines of one kind or another. It is nevertheless apparent that the government, its problems, and the measures it undertakes to solve them are remote and shadowy, not only among the poor and uneducated but also to a large extent among these who according to socio-economic norms must be classed as at least average Americans. It has been pointed out that even legislative proposals designed specifically to satisfy some of the urgently felt needs of the people attract little close attention.[24] How much more understandable that affairs of state less obviously related to the people's immediate concerns should receive much less popular attention than seems their due.

[24] "Solutions to the problem of satisfying at least some of the needs of the people [this was written when the Townsend Plan was attracting a large following] have been proposed by experts; some solutions have been attempted through state and federal legislation; some have been widely publicized. But there is ample evidence that a large proportion of the population, particularly the lower cultural groups with the greatest need, is either unaware of possible remedies offered or, being aware of them, knows little about them or is uninterested. It is not easy for a busy, worried, uneducated person, already harassed with pressing problems of his own that demand immediate solution, to see the significance in his life of a certain foreign policy, a certain agricultural subsidy, or a certain regulation of the stock exchange." Reprinted by permission from *The Psychology of Social Movements*, by Hadley Cantril, published by John Wiley & Sons, New York, 1941.

Granted that these affairs of state are exceedingly complex, and that dealing with them demands not only highly specialized knowledge and expert judgment but also a perspective on the future that cannot characterize the individual as it must the institution of government, it may still be argued that something less than a thoughtful effort has been made to inform the people about the meaning of their country's postwar international role. Much of the news is presented, probably unintentionally as well as intentionally, in such a way as to reinforce existing outmoded frames of reference. This appears to have been the case regarding the British loan. It may account in part for the immense importance people attach to our possession of bomb "secrets." "Informing the public" may call for more than simply talking and writing at people harder than before but in the same ways. It may be not only that the people need more information about specific social and political issues, but that they need to see these issues in meaningful contexts that make their relevance clear and that allow them to grasp the implications of alternate courses of action. In the field of international relations this calls for a more adequate analysis of the world situation and a deeper understanding of the way people think about such matters than has thus far been demonstrated by those responsible for public information.

There is doubtless a considerable amount of conflict and confusion of thought among the country's leaders themselves about the nature of the world situation and the role the United States should play. But even while they seek to clarify things for themselves, it is vital that they make every effort to close the serious gap which exists between what they are thinking and trying to do and the information and understanding of these matters on the part of the people. Just how this can be done is admittedly a difficult and complicated problem. But it is clear that the attempt must be made. Moreover, the general objectives can be stated.

In the first place, this study points to the need for greater effort and skill in focusing the attention of large segments of the public on the problems of our relations with other countries and on the related problems of the control of atomic energy. This needs to be done in such a way that the citizen will see that he has a vital personal stake in constructive solutions of the problems in our relations with other nations.

Along with this focusing of attention and securing psychological involvement must go a much more adequate grasp of the world situation than most Americans now have in their minds. The study shows that the people need a clearer perception of the world as a total dynamic situation of interacting parts. Perhaps the best analogous model would be that of a vast drama in which the nations are the actors. This would require that they gain a minimum of understanding of the dominant motives, goals, and perspectives and expectations of at least the major nation-actors of the drama, including our own.

If a substantial portion of the American public could be given even a moderately good comprehension of the dynamic world situation, including an understanding of the perspectives of each of the major nations, there would be a reasonably good basis for accomplishing a third objective, namely, a clear conception of the role required of the United States in the situation if we are to strive most effectively for the kind of world community that will make possible the maintenance and extension of democratic values. Intelligent opinions on specific action proposals concerning tariff policies, loans, military plans, reconstruction plans in various areas of the world, and so forth, cannot be formulated unless the relevance of such actions for a clearly conceived role in a clearly structured situation is understood by the people. Many of the contradictions and inconsistencies in the thinking of Americans as revealed by the surveys reported in this book point to the lack of this kind of clarity in the people's thinking.

It goes without saying that the general kind of approach to public information suggested here lends itself as well to abuse as it does to constructive use for the general good. A biased or loaded analysis of the situation and definition of our role could lead to actions in the interests of special groups and contrary to the general national interests. The best protection against a misuse of this approach is an unremitting effort to insure that competing diagnoses of the situation and conceptions of our national role be thoroughly examined and their action implications and probable impact on international relations carefully weighed.

If the approach to the public information on international relations we are suggesting here leads to the conclusion that the task is of a magnitude beyond our capacity, it should be remembered that the creation of a stable world community is a matter of the survival of human society, and that the creation of this community rests in the final analysis on an enlightened admixture of self-interest and social responsibility in the thinking and action of the peoples who will compose this community. No cost in money and effort is too great for the accomplishment of this state of mind and spirit.

APPENDIX A · ILLUSTRATIVE INTERVIEWS

In ORDER to acquaint the reader more fully with the interviewing method used in the intensive survey, three interviews are here presented as they were recorded by the interviewers. *They are not to be thought of as showing "typical" opinions* of any particular segment of the population. They are meant only to show the questions that were asked in all the interviews, and the amount of detail with which the answers were recorded. The examples had to be limited to three because of considerations of space, and these three were chosen arbitrarily from among twenty-five records drawn at random from the files.

The first interview was taken in August, the other two in June 1946.

INTERVIEW I

This interview was with a 67-year-old farmer in Virginia, whose 1945 income was under $500. He had not completed grade school, read no newspaper or magazine, and had no radio, although apparently he had opportunities to listen to someone else's. He had voted for Roosevelt in 1944. His sons and son-in-law had served in the armed forces during the Second World War.

Now that the war is over, how do you feel about the way the countries of the world are getting along together these days?

They are in peace. We ain't fighting. [Question repeated.] Well, I don't get around much, but from what I know they are getting along pretty good. [Why do you feel that way? [1]] Well, of course, they are getting along good in peace, but one thing is this food situation; it is awful scarce, ain't it? That is one thing that I would like to say, those countries started the war, didn't they? And if we hadn't stepped in at the right time, why we would have took a licking. I say take care of the people in this country first, and then if there is anything left, why divide it with them.

How satisfied are you with the way the United States has been getting along with other countries since the end of the war?

Oh, I think they have been getting along good as far as I know. And if we hadn't dropped in the war when we did, we would have probably been a goner now. I said that before they started fighting. [Why do you feel we are getting along?] Well, we're not fighting, are we? That is all I know.

Do you think the United States has made any mistakes in dealing with other countries since the end of the war?

Well, the only mistake I believe we made is we have been shipping too much food across to them. And the fellows back here are needing it. There ain't been no meat, lard, or sugar back here now for a long time. And another thing, they been taking grain and making liquor and beer out of it when we need it. That is one thing that is ruining the country. And a lot of folks back here are having to eat flour bread, when they ought to have corn bread. [Any other mistakes?] Well, I don't get out much and I don't read no papers, but I think if anyone should do without, they ought to be the ones. Take care of the people over here and give them what is left.

[1] The "why" questions were specified in the questionnaire. The interviewer is permitted to modify the phrasing of these "probes" to suit the context, provided the phrasing remains neutral.

What do you think is the best thing that the United States could do to help keep peace in the world?

Well, I don't know, to keep peace—to keep peace, the United States ought to trade with them, and if we got anything to let go, why give it to them hungry countries. Be good to them the best we can, and then if they jump on us, why give them a shellacking. [Anything else?] Be honest with them and not mistreat them; and if they mistreat us, why don't take anything off them.

Some people would like to see our government keep to itself and not have anything to do with the rest of the world. How do you feel about that?

Well, we couldn't do that and live right. [Why is that?] Well, part of our stuff comes from across that we don't even manufacture in this country, ain't that right? Heap of times we have stuff to sell and they need it and they have stuff that we want. I believe in dealing with them. We ought to use their money and they ought to use ours. [Any other reason why we should deal with the rest of the world?] Well, we got to deal with the rest of the world and help them. If we were to cut this island off, where would we get our rice and coffee? We get most of that from other countries, don't we?

Some people say we should use our Army and Navy to make other countries do what we think they should. How would you feel about that?

You mean use the Army and Navy to make them do what we think? [Yes.] I don't know what kind of an answer to give you. I believe all the nations that we whupped should come under our rule; and not let them make any artillery so we won't have to fight them again. I believe in making them do what we want. But a nation we haven't had anything to do with, I don't believe in pestering them until they have pestered us. [Why do you think the countries we whipped should come under our law?] To keep them from fighting us again. To keep them from making artillery. The grudge is still in them and if they get a chance they will fight. Like old Germany the last war. If they had made her do what they should have last time she wouldn't have been fighting us.

How about some of the other countries? Do you think the English Government is trying to cooperate with the rest of the world as much as it can?

I don't know, I don't take no papers. I would just like to leave that one off. [From what you do know and have heard?] I don't know, I don't read none and haven't been around much, but I did hear back yonder that she was trying to undermine the United States. But I don't know if that was so or not. So I wouldn't want to say on account of that.

How about the United States? Do you think we can count on the English Government being friendly with us?

I don't know. I'd be dubious of that; I'd watch her. [Why is that?] Well, I have heard some talk of the English, but I don't know how true it was and I wouldn't want to say much about her. When I don't know something I don't like to fool with it.

You probably know that Congress recently voted to lend a large amount of money to England. How do you feel about that?

I don't believe they should have loaned her that much. [Would you have lent her any?] Well, I don't know, I don't believe I would. [Why?] I would be dubious, she might take a turn on us and use the money to make artillery and use it on us. See there what Russia did, see what we did for her, and where would she have been, if it hadn't been for us? And then when it come time to make peace why we couldn't hardly make peace with her. If I was the one loaning the money, I would have my own men go in the country and see what they did with it and see that they didn't use it to make artillery with it and if they were I wouldn't let them have it.

Do you think we have anything to gain from making the loan?

I don't know that.

How about Russia? Do you think the Russian Government is trying to cooperate with the rest of the world as much as it can?

Well, I ain't heard nothing about Russia lately. They give us some trouble to start with, but I ain't heard nothing of her lately; but I would keep my eye on her. [Why do you think they should?] Well, the way she done after the war. They were hard to settle with and she might take a turn and give trouble some day.

How about the United States? Do you think we can count on the Russian Government being friendly with us?

Well, I don't know about that. My idea is that she will be friendly for a while and then if she gets a chance to fight us she will be ready to fight. She was hard to settle with. [Why do you think so?] Well, all I know is she would be ready to fight us in a minute. As good as we were to her, and then she was so hard to settle with. But she ain't give no trouble from what I can hear.

There's talk now about the United States lending a large amount of money to Russia. How do you feel about that?

I wouldn't loan her a dollar. She was so hard to settle with after the war; I wouldn't loan her a dime. The way she done after the war is what I got against her. If I pick you up out of the water when you are up to your neck and then when I get you out you try to push me in, why I don't feel so good to you. I got no dependence in Russia. She is a sneak, the way I got her down. I'd just be afraid when she got ready to pay us back it would be in bullets.

Do you think we have anything to gain from making the loan?

I think we would have a lot to lose in the end of it. I would trade with Russia and be good to her, but I wouldn't lend her a dime and I would depend on fighting her every day.

Have you been following the news about the United Nations organization during the last few months?

No, I ain't.

As you see it, what is the main thing the UNO [2] is set up to do?

Don't know. Don't know what it is.[3]

Do you think it would be possible to organize the nations of the world in the same way the states in this country are organized, with a government over them all to make laws that they would all have to obey?

I wouldn't like to say nothing about that. [Well, what's your own opinion?] I don't know, I believe every nation should organize herself and let the rest go. I believe when we whup a nation we ought to put her under our government but let the balance of them go. Those we don't whup, why, leave them alone. I don't know, I don't want to go into that too much. I have studied that right much, but I don't know.

How would you feel about this country belonging to a world organization where we would have to follow the decisions of the majority of the nations?

I wouldn't want that. I just want my President over this island and I wouldn't want to have no other nation to have nothing to do with it. Let every island have its own president.

[2] The initials "UNO" were used in the interview questions rather than UN, as the former seemed to be more widely understood.

[3] The other questions in which the United Nations was mentioned were not asked of respondents who were not familiar with the organization. For those questions, see the next example.

Do you think the discovery of the atomic bomb has made it easier or harder to keep peace in the world?

Made it easier. [Why is that?] Well, they know if they raise any cain, why they are going to get destroyed right now and I am in favor of no other nation knowing about it. When the bomb fell, we had peace. I don't want them to make it to fight us with. I wouldn't put no confidence in no nation under the sun to have it.

How worried do you think people in this country are about the atomic bomb?

They are all for it, peace was made with it and there was big talk when it happened. [Question repeated.] No, they ain't unless they know that some other country gets the patent. The country is pleased with it.

How about yourself?

No, all I am worried about is that some other country might get the patent. If we had had the atomic bomb, the war wouldn't have lasted six months. I never was so proud of something in my life as I was when it fell. I'm just afeered some other nations might get the patent.

How long do you think it will be before the other countries are able to make atomic bombs?

I don't know; I wouldn't know that. I didn't know how long it took them to make this one.

Do you think we will be able to work out a defense against the bomb before other countries learn how to make it?

I don't know, but I suppose if they could make it they could patent something to take care of that.

Do you think there is real danger that atomic bombs will ever be used against the United States?

I couldn't tell you. Afeered it will. If they get the privilege they would use it, but if the United States don't give them that privilege, they never would make it, I don't reckon.

Do you think the discovery of the atomic bomb makes any difference in the size of the Army we need?

Don't look like they would need none, hardly. If they had enough atomic bombs, they could use them to clean out a nation. The man that made that bomb was a man after my own heart. I love him. I don't care if he was a nigger. I'd love his neck.

How about the Navy? Does it make any difference in the size of Navy we will need?

No, we don't need as much Navy, don't look like, with the bomb. [Why?] Well, it gives men a chance to be somewhere else. Don't need as many with the bomb.

What about the Air Force? Does it make any difference in the size of Air Force we will need?

No, I believe the Air Force should be right there. They are the only ones that can throw the bombs and we need plenty of them. They need to be training them every day. The Navy can't throw them bombs. But I believe in keeping plenty of soldiers all the time. We ought to have plenty of bombs and artillery ready all the time, and have plenty of grub stuff laid up and be ready for them. We like to not got ready for them this time.

Have you heard anything about the atomic bomb tests the Navy made last month in the Pacific?

I heard they let one off, but I haven't heard what happened. We don't have a radio and I haven't heard what happened. It was let off in the sea, wasn't it? Last count I took, they hadn't figured up what damage it had done.

Do you happen to know how many bombs were exploded?

No, I don't know.

Did you expect the bomb (or bombs) to destroy most of the ships or just a few of them?

I don't know nothing about that.

Did you expect the bomb (or bombs) to be as destructive against these ships as it was against the Japanese cities?
Yeh, I expected it to do just as much damage one place as another. It destroys everything for eight miles, doesn't it? It ought to do as much damage one place as another.

We're interested in knowing how people keep up with the news on the atomic bomb. Where would you say you've gotten most of your information on the atomic bomb?
I listened to it over the radio. They tell what it done, I listen to Lowell Thomas.

Have you read anything about the bomb in the newspapers?
No.

Have you read anything about the bomb in magazines?
No, I don't read any of them, but we do take some and from the way they said Russia was holding out and wouldn't settle with us, if it hadn't been for the atomic bomb we would have had to fight them then and there. That is the talk in this country.

Have you seen any movies or newsreels about the atomic bomb?
No—never go to movies.

Have you talked it over with other people?
No, I don't know as I have.

INTERVIEW II

This respondent was 24 years old, a recent graduate of an Eastern university, and employed by a Pennsylvania concern as a chemical engineer at a salary of between $3000 and $4000. He read a daily paper, *Time*, *Life*, *Saturday Evening Post*, and *Colliers*, and numerous engineering journals, and listened to radio discussions of international affairs. He had voted in 1944 for the Republican Presidential candidate.

He was living in an apartment he shared with a young man his own age. The interviewer noted that "the apartment looked like a cross between a fraternity house and a recording studio." Of more relevance, perhaps, is the interviewer's notation that the respondent "had well-developed, previously-thought-out opinions on all questions asked. I had some difficulty in keeping up with his rapid flow of ideas. Each answer developed itself, with very few probes."

Now that the war is over, how do you feel about the way the countries of the world are getting along together these days?
I think they're doing a rather stinking job. During wartime, their cooperation was primarily due to a desire to defeat a common enemy—not because they believed in the same things. Now that the enemy is defeated, each one fights for what he believed in all along. Russia has gone back to Russian expansionism, using the Communist Party as a stalking horse. It isn't that they believe in Communism at all. The United States and Britain are still playing their game of economic imperialism, but not as much as before. France is less of a power than it was, but still tries to throw its weight around in international politics; however, France won't count as in the past. I'm not surprised that we aren't getting along as well as we did during the war.

How satisfied are you with the way the United States has been getting along with other countries since the war ended?
Well, we've always been pretty goodhearted. We've been rich, we've given to worthy causes, and are still doing so. The biggest trouble is our lack of a coherent foreign policy. We have a good reputation for generosity, but a poor reputation as to what we are going to do politically, primarily because we

don't know ourselves. The real answer is to work out a positive foreign policy and follow it—a policy endorsed by both major parties, and preferably by the people as a whole.

Do you think the United States has made any mistakes in dealing with other countries since the end of the war?

Not essentially mistakes, but delaying action until the expected benefit of the action is reduced, sometimes to the point of vanishing. [For example?] This relief for Europe. We made commitments and didn't do anything about it. Because of that, the whole political organization of Europe has been held up so long that we have more chaotic conditions and worse problems than we need to have had.

What do you think is the best thing that the United States could do to help keep peace in the world?

If the UN would work, and a demonstration of workableness would be a willingness to put into practice the world government it implies, the best thing to do is to back up the UN with all we've got, which means giving up some of our sovereignty. If that doesn't work—and the only reason it wouldn't is Russian obstructionism—then we should organize the UN without Russia, include the rest of the world that agrees with us, and fight for the purposes we think right. That's loading dynamite for a future war, but I don't think Russia wants war. If they see we'll go ahead without them—that is, call their bluff—they'll come along with us. That may be the only way to get them in. Also, because Russia responds to force, keep a strong armed force in this country.

Some people would like to see our government keep to itself and not have anything to do with the rest of the world. How do you feel about that?

I think it would be a complete mistake. The world is getting smaller. That's an old saw, but it's true.

*Some people say we should use our Army and Navy to make
other countries do what we think they should. How would
you feel about that?*

No. [Why, would you say?] I don't think that's a good idea,
primarily because a policeman is always hated. If we try to
police the world, it is only by dictating to other countries, and
we preach democracy. The only way is to convince the other
countries we are right. We're occupying two enemy countries.
In Germany, the major powers are dictating policy, and the
Germans do as they are told. When we pull out, they'll do as
they please, probably become militaristic and vengeful. In
Japan, we are telling them what to do but at the same time
educating them in democracy. When we pull out of Japan,
they'll continue in that pattern. The four-power occupation of
Germany was a complete mistake. There should be complete
collaboration at the top level, and no division of the country.
I don't blame Eisenhower, and I don't credit MacArthur;
circumstances in Germany prevented the right type of occupation.

*How about some of the other countries? Do you think the
English Government is trying to cooperate with the rest of
the world as much as it can?*

The British have two problems: one is to maintain their empire, which is partly democratic, the British Commonwealth
of Nations, and partly an imperialistic hodge-podge; to maintain this empire, because, without the empire, Britain, because
of its size, would sink to the level of a minor power with a
much decreased standard of living. Secondly, they do want a
democratic world and I think they are doing all they can to
bring it about except where such action would conflict, where
it would bring about sacrifice of their empire. A perfectly
understandable position.

How about the United States? Do you think we can count on the English Government being friendly with us?
Yes. They always have been since the War of 1812. Our foreign policies coincide, our heritage is the same, we have remarkably parallel interests. In fact, parallel enough to be used as evidence of monopolistic practice [laugh], if there were laws against international political monopoly.

There's talk now about the United States lending a large amount of money to England. How do you feel about that?
Well, to a certain extent, I think we are suckers, not for making the loan—that's necessary—but for getting nothing in return, not even a token, no commitments as to future policy. However, if we didn't make the loan, England might go into an advanced stage of Socialism, or even Communism, although I doubt that. Helping them is like helping us, which is the best reason for making the loan.

Do you think we have anything to gain from making the loan?
Britain controls a lot of world trade. If Britain was poor, our export trade would suffer. On the political side, Britain has been virtually our ally. It's a good smart policy to see that our friends are well off. Making the loan presents the problem of what justification there is for not making the loan to anyone else that comes along.

How about Russia? Do you think the Russian Government is trying to cooperate with the rest of the world as much as it can?
No, completely no! Russia is expanding by any means it can take. They're not necessarily expanding Communism, though they use it as an excuse, as a stalking horse. [How do you mean?] I don't think they're interested in communizing the world. They just want men in power in neighboring states

who will do what Russia says. It's imperialist expansion, disguised.

How about the United States? Do you think we can count on the Russian Government being friendly with us?

Only when it suits Russia's purpose. They're out for Russia, and to hell with the rest of the world. They may go along with us to keep us quiet, while pursuing their own activities, which may not agree with our ideas.

There's talk now about the United States lending a large amount of money to Russia. How do you feel about that?

Under the present conditions, no. If Russia would permit travel of our correspondents through Russian-occupied lands and perhaps through Russia itself, and if they make some specific commitments which we have a way of checking—as to the planned use of the money, and what their foreign policy will be—I'd consider it, but just consider it. They need the money because of the ravages of war. If the ways in which they would use the money are not harmful to us, but merely to rebuild, we could lend it, but I fear the money would be used to continue to finance their imperialistic expansionism, which is exactly what we don't want. That expansionism is the real bone of contention between us. They're trying to take over Asia and eastern Europe as their economic province, excluding the United States. They will stop their attacks only if we can show them to be unprofitable.

Do you think we have anything to gain from making the loan?

Only under the conditions I mentioned. If they stop making governments subservient to Moscow, and if the Russian people are told it's our money, not Russian money. Not like with lend-lease equipment. Did you know that parts of the Russian Army were told that the jeeps and trucks were Russian made? [I hadn't heard that.] The relief should be clearly coming

from America. We should get credit with the people for it.
Have you been following the news about the United Nations organization during the last few months?
Yes.
As you see it, what is the main thing the UNO is set up to do?
If nothing else, to be a debating hall, but Russia is trying to gag it by using her veto power. In theory, it has a police power in that it can call on the armed forces or economic action of its members. But since adherence to its economic policies or the furnishing of military power is subject to the discretion of the power involved, I don't think either one will amount to anything if a violent crisis develops. The UN will function only as long as the major powers want it to.
How do you feel about the general idea of having an organization like the UNO?
It hasn't fulfilled all my hopes, but it has fulfilled my expectations. It's exceedingly hard to get nations to surrender their sovereignty. The two nations that resist this the most are Russia and the United States. Until that's done, no world government will have real authority.
Do you think the United States has given in too much or has had its own way too much in the UNO?
I think we have given in to Russia a little too much. [On any specific points?] Yes, in regard to the governments of the countries around Russia. We protested, but did nothing. They are not representative governments; they are controlled by Russia. Those countries are little more than additional Soviets in the U.S.S.R., whether or not their people wanted it.
Do you think the United States ought to have more say than the other big countries, or should they all have the same?
That's a tough one to answer. I think the United States should have more say than France, which is not a major power equal

to the United States, Great Britain, or Russia. In world politics, it's the amount of force a country can assemble that determines the power the country has. This country has more force than its population or area indicates. China is not ten times as powerful as the United States, but has ten times the population and area; it's not as important in its present state of development. [Do you think then that the United States should have more say?] Let's put it this way. If you don't give them equal vote, how can you decide who gets what vote? Population or acreage are meaningless. The real criterion is the war-making potential. The vote should be based on that, but that can't be figured. [Then you think—?] The big powers should have equal say. Probably the United States and Russia are the two most important and powerful nations, but the British Empire, taken as a whole, is a third equal.

How successful do you think the UNO will be in keeping peace among the countries?

That's a crystal-ball question. If the UN takes unto itself the powers of a real governing body, by small steps, and if the nations of the world agree to that, and then concede that powers should be transferred to the world government, and want peace. But as it is now, with Russia opposed to the UN having real power, it's not a governing body and can't prevent war.

Suppose the United States and another country had a disagreement which they couldn't settle; do you think the UNO should have the power to tell both of them what ought to be done?

If it had equal power to settle disputes between any two countries, then we can't make an exception for the United States. That's the problem in making a world government. Each country must surrender some sovereignty to a central government, which should be representative of all of them.

Do you think it would be possible to organize the nations of the world in the same way the states in this country are organized, with a government over them all to make laws that they would all have to obey?

I think it would be possible. [Why do you think so?] It is necessary, eventually, but I'm afraid we won't have it until after the next war. The present states won't surrender any sovereignty until it's too late to prevent the war. The UNO is based on the idea that you can get every nation to agree. I don't think that is possible at present where they have to surrender authority. For example, the United States doesn't want China to tell us what to do. We don't understand their way of life, and they don't understand ours. The only way to do it is for the United States and the British Commonwealth of Nations, and possibly France, the Dutch, Belgium—those countries with whom we have a common heritage, political organization, and aspirations—these nations should federate. But the organization should not be closed, but open to the admission of a new member when the suitable number, say two-thirds, agree; provided the people of the country want to get in. Only by starting with complete federal power and taking in those who will agree, will you get agreement to abide by the laws of the federation. The biggest danger of such a setup is that it would stop in mid-course, that it would organize half the world against the other half. But if that occurred, it means there's a fundamental opposition of ideals that would result in war anyhow. [After answering the next question, the respondent asked to go back to this one, and added the following.] Regarding a federated government, it is important that there be no customs barriers, that there be economic unity. In order to accomplish that, we'll suffer some loss in our standard of living. That would be unfortunate, but war would be more unfortunate.

How would you feel about this country belonging to a world organization where we would have to follow the decisions of the majority of the nations?

I'm all for it, as my preceding answer shows, provided the organization is essentially similar to our federal government, where the people who run the government are not a small group, or ruling party. There must be no miscarriage of democracy.

Do you think this world organization should have armed forces to carry out its decisions if necessary?

Yes. [Why?] The present arrangement can easily be hamstrung by the refusal of any major power that commands a significant military force to donate their forces. A veto can be used if one major nation is a party to a dispute. If the UN has its own army, there's not the invitation to a general war, there is an integrated army ready to move.

Do you think the discovery of the atomic bomb has made it easier or harder to keep peace in the world?

Harder, because it puts a tremendous initial advantage at the disposal of the attacker. It increases immeasurably the possibility of a blitzkrieg, and therefore there is a strong temptation for a single man to suddenly launch a war.

How worried do you think people in this country are about the atomic bomb?

Some people are very worried, hysterically so. The majority of them are not worried, primarily because they haven't thought about what it means. I don't think one bomb will wipe out a city. The concrete air raid shelters in the Japanese cities were gutted but not destroyed. A steel city like New York would suffer terrible damage and loss of life, but I don't think it would destroy the city. Of course, more powerful bombs can be built, probably have been by now.

How about yourself? (How worried are you?)

As long as our government is continuing atomic research so we won't be caught by new and more drastic developments, I'm not particularly worried, although it is inviting for an aggressor to launch a war that might knock out a country before it knew it was being attacked, or at least destroy its power to defend. I don't think an atomic attack will defeat this country, but, followed by a regular war, it could. The United States has never been defeated, but it is not invincible. Let's call it "apprehension" rather than "worry." It hasn't given me the jitters, but it is something to think about.

How long do you think it will be before the other countries are able to make atomic bombs?

Russia has been working on nuclear physics as long as we have. Probably not over a year or two more and they'll have it; they may have it already. As for the other countries, even if they had it, they don't have the productive facilities to use it effectively. Those that might develop the bomb are either friendly to us, or not capable of utilizing it, except for Russia.

Do you think the secret of the bomb should be turned over to the UNO, or should the United States try to keep the secret itself?

Not as the UN is at present constituted. It's only a debating society without real power. Control should be turned over to a real world government. If we had a true world government, it would be impossible to keep any secret from it; it would automatically have at its disposal all the information available to its members.

Do you think we will be able to work out a defense against the bomb before other countries learn how to make it?

No. [Why do you think that?] The atomic bomb can be carried in small missiles, and these can be self-propelled by rockets. They can be fired at high altitudes. They are undetectable until they hit. There are no devices that could be put into operation fast enough upon detection, if detection were possible.

Do you think there is real danger that atomic bombs will ever be used against the United States?

Yes. Exactly the same danger as there is of getting into another war. If we're in a war, the atomic bomb will be used against us.

Do you think the discovery of the atomic bomb makes any difference in the size of the Army we need?

Size no, character yes. The United States has been against peacetime military training. The atomic bomb now makes that necessary. In an atomic war there is no time to train men for the armed services; they must know beforehand how to become an army. If we have a large recently trained reserve, we need a small corps of specialists, a small professional army such as we've always had. But we must have, in addition, a continuously trained reserve such as we never had in the past.

How about the Navy? Does it make any difference in the size of Navy we will need?

The same answer to that one. I'd preserve the entire Navy as a stand-by—there are ways now of preventing the equipment from decaying. I'd maintain a small active Navy, but keep the rest in stand-by condition. We'd have a small professional Navy and a highly trained organized reserve. My point is that there will be no time to train for the next war. The primary assault will be against the United States because we are the arsenal of the democracies.

What about the Air Force? Does it make any difference in the size of Air Force we will need?

Yes, we can use a smaller and more specialized Air Force. I don't mean a tiny Air Force. The atomic bomb is a super-bomb, but we can't use just one bomb, or one plane to win a war; we need a sizable but smaller Air Force.

Have you heard of the test the Navy plans to make of the atomic bomb?

Yes, you mean Operation Crossroads.

The Navy has collected about a hundred old ships in the South Pacific and is going to explode an atomic bomb over them. Do you expect the bomb will destroy most of these ships or just a few of them?

Probably some will be destroyed by their own ammunition going off, set off by the heat wave. I don't think it'll destroy many ships. In actual battle conditions, it would destroy the crews of all the ships, but I don't think it would destroy the ships.

Do you expect the bomb to be as destructive against these ships as it was against Japanese cities?

No. [Why not?] Because the Japanese cities were destroyed principally by fire which followed the initial concussion and heat wave. Ships won't burn, and they are isolated by water.

We're interested in knowing how people keep up with the news on the atomic bomb. Where would you say you've gotten most of your information on the atomic bomb?

The Smyth Report. Also a few books and pamphlets, magazines, principally *Time Magazine*, and newspapers. The Smyth Report gives the bulk of the information.

Have you heard anything about the bomb over the radio?

Sure—they're always making references to it, but never say much about the workings of the bomb. It's pitched to the average level of understanding, that it is a super-bomb.

Have you read anything about the bomb in the newspapers?

Most of that is a discussion of what to do about the bomb, the control of atomic energy, rather than the mechanism of the bomb.

Have you read anything about the bomb in magazines?

All the periodicals discuss the governmental rather than the scientific end of the bomb. The Smyth Report is concerned entirely with the scientific end.

Which of these three (radio, newspapers, or magazines) do you trust the most for information about the atomic bomb?

Magazines—they're much less sensational.

Have you seen any movies or newsreels about the atomic bomb?

Yes, of the test in New Mexico.

Have you talked it over with other people?

Yes.

Would you say you do that rather often or just now and then?

Now and then, but thoroughly.

In general, which of these ways of getting information has given you the best idea of how destructive the atomic bomb is?

Of course, pictures of Hiroshima dramatize the destructiveness more than the imagination can be built up by reading about it. We don't appreciate how destructive it is from any source.

Which of all these ways has been most important in helping you make up your mind about who should have the secret of the bomb?

None of them. The most important way is to think about what I'd do if I had the bomb. This is colored, however, by what I have read and discussed. My opinion not to give control to the UN is based on a strong conviction that the UN doesn't have sufficient force at its disposal to maintain peace, if peace is not desired by one of the major powers; and I don't trust Russian intentions in regard to the UN.

INTERVIEW III

This man was a skilled worker in Scranton, Pennsylvania, with an annual income (for 1945) in the $2000–$3000 bracket. He was 56 years old, had had a high-school education, read a daily paper but no magazines, and owned a radio. His parents were of English birth; he, himself, a native Pennsylvanian. He had voted in the 1944 Presidential election, but declined to say for which candidate.

Now that the war is over, how do you feel about the way the countries of the world are getting along together these days?
I think they are all getting along O.K., with the exception of Russia. The other countries seem to be pulling together as well as possible, trying to work out ways to get the world back to normal. Russia seems to be the only one causing any rift in the plans.

How satisfied are you with the way the United States has been getting along with other countries since the war ended?
Quite satisfied. I think the United States is doing everything humanly possible to bring peace to the world.

Do you think the United States has made any mistakes in dealing with other countries since the end of the war?
I wouldn't know. I think it's too early to say whether or not mistakes have been made.

What do you think is the best thing that the United States could do to help keep peace in the world?
I think if the United States carries on as she is now, she can do a lot for world peace. [Why do you feel this way?] Because I think the United States has the interest of the world at heart, and she is proving her friendship by feeding and clothing the destitute nations.

Some people would like to see our government keep to it-self and not have anything to do with the rest of the world. How do you feel about that?

No, I don't think so because a country that keeps to itself, if they are in need, who would they turn to for help in case of a crisis? It's the same as with a person.

Some people say we should use our Army and Navy to make other countries do what we think they should. How would you feel about that?

Only in case of necessity—by that, I mean if some harm was being done to our country. Other countries have a right to their own opinions, the same as this country. We certainly wouldn't want the army and navy of other countries coming in here and telling us what to do, even though what we are doing does not meet with their approval.

How about some of the other countries? Do you think the English Government is trying to cooperate with the rest of the world as much as it can?

I think they are with this country, but not with all countries. [In what ways?] I would rather not state.

How about the United States? Do you think we can count on the English Government being friendly with us?

I think so. [Why?] Well, England and the United States have always been friendly, and I can see no reason why their attitude should change.

There's talk now about the United States lending a large amount of money to England. How do you feel about that?

I think if England really needs the money, we should lend it to them, but I feel that there are a great many other countries much worse off than England. The people in many of the European countries are facing starvation, and I would prefer to see the money go to relieve human suffering. I think the only reason England wants this money is to rebuild her country. Other countries were just as hard hit, but we aren't always reading about them asking for loans. I think that England should prove their need before any money is lent to them.

Do you think we have anything to gain from making the loan?

Personally, I don't think we have anything to gain. [Why?] Well, they owed us millions before the war which was hanging since the last war and we have never collected it. It would probably be the same if we loaned them now, so we would stand a loss instead of gaining anything.

How about Russia? Do you think the Russian Government is trying to cooperate with the rest of the world as much as it can?

I do not. [In what ways?] Well, from her action in the United Nations conferences. She wants to stay aloof. And it looks to me as though Russia wants world power.

How about the United States? Do you think we can count on the Russian Government being friendly with us?

To a certain extent. [Why do you feel that way?] I feel that she will remain friendly as long as she wants some help from us, but in eight or ten years, when Russia is on her feet, she would not hesitate to sever the friendship. As I said before, Russia hopes to gain world power and she will get it even if it means another war.

There's talk now about the United States lending a large amount of money to Russia. How do you feel about that?

I can't answer that. I don't know any of the particulars. [How do you feel about it?] I don't feel that we should. [Why?] I feel that we will only be digging our own graves. It will be another case of Japan. We supplied them with all our scrap metal with the hope of keeping them pacified, but in the end they fired it all back at us in the form of bullets. I think this same thing will happen if we don't take a firm stand with Russia.

Do you think we have anything to gain from making the loan?

No, not a thing. In fact, we would lose a whole lot if they used the money to prepare themselves for a future war.

Have you been following the news about the United Nations organization during the last few months?

To some extent.

As you see it, what is the main thing the UNO is set up to do?

To bring about world peace.

How do you feel about the general idea of having an organization like the UNO?

I think it's a good idea because it's trying to bring out a friendly feeling from one country to another. It establishes a closer relationship between countries.

How satisfied are you with the way the UNO has worked out so far?

Well, I think there is a lot to be done yet. I think it is still in the organization stage and they haven't really started rolling yet.

Do you think the United States has given in too much or has had its own way too much in the UNO?

I wouldn't say either one.

Do you think the United States ought to have more say than the other big countries, or should they all have the same?

I think all the large countries should have the same say. [Why?] Well, everybody—especially the three largest countries, should be on an equal basis, with no one having more to say or do than the other.

How successful do you think the UNO will be in keeping peace among the countries?

I don't know. I think it's too early to say. If they can lay down their plans and if all nations follow them religiously, then it will be successful; but if they squabble among themselves and if countries' representatives get up and walk out mad, as Russia has been doing, then I think it will be doomed to failure. Time alone will tell.

Suppose the United States and another country had a disagreement which they couldn't settle; do you think the UNO should have the power to tell both of them what ought to be done?

Yes indeed. That's the purpose of the UNO.

Do you think it would be possible to organize the nations of the world in the same way the states in this country are organized, with a government over them all to make laws that they would all have to obey?

No, I do not. It would never work out. [Why do you feel that way?] Because those countries have been self-governing for so many years that I don't believe it would ever be possible to organize them under one government. That would certainly cause war among the nations over there.

How would you feel about this country belonging to a world organization where we would have to follow the decisions of the majority of the nations?

I don't think I'd like it. [Why?] I don't want dictators. [How do you mean?] Well, a group of small nations may want to do something that we wouldn't want to go along on but as a group they will vote as a unit for it and we would have to go along whether we wanted to or not.

Do you think the discovery of the atomic bomb has made it easier or harder to keep peace in the world?

I think the bomb has made it harder to keep the peace. [Why do you think so?] Well, it has just kept the other nations unsettled trying to get hold of it.

How worried do you think people in this country are about the atomic bomb?

I think everyone has some concern about it. There seems to be great fear that other countries may get hold of it.

How about yourself?

Not too much. [Why so?] I feel that the government will work out some method of defense.

How long do you think it will be before the other countries are able to make atomic bombs?

That's a question. [How long would you say?] I couldn't answer. I haven't any idea.

Do you think the secret of the bomb should be turned over to the UNO, or should the United States try to keep the secret itself?

I think the United States should keep the secret to itself. [Why?] Well, if it would be turned over to the UNO all the member nations would have the information. Then, there would be the chance that some nation might drop out from the UNO and they would have the information and still would be nonmembers of the UNO.

Do you think we will be able to work out a defense against the bomb before other countries learn how to make it?

We may and we may not. I am not certain that any defense can be worked out, but I am placing my trust in these great masterminds that are working on it now to develop some defense measures and that it will be done before any other countries get to know about the bomb.

Do you think there is real danger that atomic bombs will ever be used against the United States?

I don't feel that there is any immediate danger, but I most certainly feel that they will be used if there is ever another war. [Why do you feel that way?] Well, we almost got them in the last war. From what I read, Germany would have had the secret in a few months when the war ended, and we can be sure that they would have used them on us if the war had continued, say, another six months or so.

Do you think the discovery of the atomic bomb makes any difference in the size of the Army we need?

No, I don't think so. [Why?] Well, I said I don't think so, but then I guess that is a decision for the military brains of the country, and who am I to offer an opinion on it?

How about the Navy? Does it make any difference in the size of Navy we will need?

Well, I think so far as the size of the Army and Navy are concerned, everything will depend on the outcome of the bomb tests that are to be made out in the Pacific this summer.

What about the Air Force? Does it make any difference in the size of Air Force we will need?

Well, I think the size of the Air Force will also depend on the tests.

The Navy has collected about a hundred old ships in the South Pacific and is going to explode an atomic bomb over them. Do you expect the bomb will destroy most of these ships or just a few of them? [4]

Yes, I do, most of them. We had an example of what it can do when they were dropped on Hiroshima. When a bomb can destroy a whole city it surely will destroy a hundred ships.

Do you expect the bomb to be as destructive against these ships as it was against the Japanese cities?

Yes. The bomb seems to be so powerful that I think it can destroy anything. Of course, all we know about the bomb is what the government wanted us to know, and the censorship was strict.

We're interested in knowing how people keep up with the

[4] The question, "Have you heard of the test the Navy plans to make of the atomic bomb?" was omitted because the respondent had already spontaneously indicated his awareness of the project.

news on the atomic bomb. Where would you say you've got-
ten most of your information on the atomic bomb?
Oh, from the newspapers and the radio.
Have you read anything about the bomb in magazines?
No.
Which of the two (radio or newspapers) do you trust the
most for information about the atomic bomb?
The radio, I believe. [Why?] Because we seem to get the
opinions of so many different commentators and news analysts.
Have you seen any movies or newsreels about the atomic
bomb?
I have seen it in the newsreel.
Have you talked it over with other people?
Yes, now and again.
In general, which of these ways of getting information has
given you the best idea of how destructive the atomic bomb
is?
The newsreel.
Which of all these ways has been most important in helping
you make up your mind about who should have the secret of
the bomb?
I think they have all been important.

APPENDIX B · TABULAR MATERIAL

THE MAIN PURPOSE of this appendix is to present the details of those survey questions and answers which have been referred to directly or indirectly in the text. No attempt has been made, either in the text or in the appendix, to review all the questions dealt with in our surveys, since it has been necessary to limit the size of the book considerably. Included in the appendix are those relatively few tables from other surveys that have been mentioned in the text. Most of them have been taken from the fortnightly digest *Opinion News*, published by the National Opinion Research Center, University of Chicago, or from the journal *Public Opinion Quarterly*, published by the Princeton University Press. A few are from the files of the Survey Research Center of the University of Michigan. All are reproduced here by permission of survey agencies responsible for them. Acknowledgment of their courtesies is made in the authors' preface.

The Samples

Extensive survey. The sample for this survey was drawn by the "quota" method. In June (before the Bikini test) 3090 people were interviewed, in August (after the test) 2984 people. Each group constituted a representative cross-section of the adult population of the United States. The relations of opinion to level of information shown in the tables are those found in June (see "Level of Information About World Affairs" below). In showing the relations of one opinion to another, the June and August samples have been combined.

Intensive survey. This sample was drawn by a method known as "stratified random sampling," which is described in some detail in the original report, to which the reader interested in survey techniques is referred.[1] In June 585 people were interviewed, in August 592. Each group constituted a representative cross-section of the adult population of the United States. In the following tables, in showing the relations between one attitude and another, the relations between attitude and level of information, and the "reasons" respondents gave for their attitudes, the two samples have been combined unless otherwise indicated.

Order in Which the Tables Are Presented

References were omitted from the text to page numbers or table numbers in the appendix, because it was thought that these would needlessly interfere with readability. The tables have been grouped under a few headings that follow the order of the discussion as closely as practicable; under each heading the tables are grouped according to their origins (extensive survey, intensive survey, and other surveys), and so do not follow precisely the order in which they are taken up in the text. Most of the tables are accompanied by explanatory notes showing the relation of one table to another, so that the appendix has a certain continuity of its own.

Special Characteristics of the Intensive-Survey Tables

"With qualifications or uncertainty." The interviewing and analytical methods of the intensive survey are described briefly in Chapter 1. As mentioned there, efforts are made to preserve

[1] *Public Reaction to the Atomic Bomb and World Affairs.* Cornell University, Ithaca, New York, April 1947.

the distinction between responses made with conviction and those made with reservations or with an evident lack of conviction. Coded as an unqualified "yes" or "no" or "approve" or "disapprove" were responses made without equivocation and supported by a reason ("I think we should lend money to England. Their country is so torn up and lots of people there need help"), and emphatically phrased responses, even though unaccompanied by supporting arguments ("Absolutely not"). Coded as responses "with qualifications or uncertainty" were those in which a reservation was expressed ("It's all right if we get the money back"), or which, while their general tenor indicated a preference, included one counterargument ("It's a big load to take on with our country in debt, but we didn't have the destruction England did, so I guess we have to do it"), or which were phrased without conviction ("I suppose it's all right"). It will be seen that in some tables these categories have not been separated; on these questions, to quote from the original report, "people did not express themselves sufficiently clearly to permit a distinction between strongly held and uncertain opinions. Such a distinction was easily made in answers to many of the questions, but could not be made on questions of the following kinds: (a) broad appraisal questions ['How do you feel about the way the countries of the world are getting along these days?']; (b) questions about a subject on which public thinking is relatively 'unstructured,' that is, one on which there has been relatively little public discussion, and which many people have not thought about [such as a question about a hypothetical form of world organization]; (c) questions that raise a conflict with some strongly held opinion [such as a question about whether the English Government is trying to cooperate with the rest of the world]."

"*Opinions not ascertained.*" Inevitably, in any large survey, the interviewers' records will contain some blanks. In the conventional poll, where the questions are few and a choice among ready-made responses is all that is usually required of the respondent, the blanks are likely to be few, and presumably will result mainly from interviewers' oversights. In our *extensive* survey, such blanks were discarded in computing the frequencies of responses, in accordance with standard practice among polling agencies. In the much longer and more complex intensive interview, in addition to the blanks that may result from oversights, there may be other unascertained answers resulting mainly from the fact that interviewers have refrained from subjecting to the entire questionnaire those respondents who have repeatedly said they "don't know," "don't think about these things." In such cases the blank is coded "opinion not ascertained" and tabulated as such. In the main text of this book where tabulations are quoted in full from the intensive survey, the "opinion not ascertained" cases have been eliminated to simplify the presentation. The effect on the percentage distribution is slight since the number of such cases is small. In this appendix, however, these cases are included in the tables and thus in some instances the reader will discover slight discrepancies between the tables in the text and their counterparts in the appendix.

Level of Information about World Affairs

Extensive Survey

In the extensive survey respondents were segregated in seven groups on the basis of the scores they made on the following questions of information:

"Do you happen to know who is the U.S. Secretary of State at the present time?" "What is his name?"

"The name of General Leslie R. Groves has been mentioned occasionally in the newspapers and over the radio in recent months. Can you tell me in what connection?"

"Do you happen to remember what country was recently charged before the United Nations organization with keeping her troops in Iran longer than she was supposed to?" "Which country?"

"Can you name the materials from which atomic energy is being made now?" "What materials?"

"Do you happen to know whether there is any plan to test the atomic bomb in the near future?" "Will you tell me what the targets are going to be in testing the bomb?"

The last question was asked in August with the tenses appropriately changed, but by August awareness of the test had increased markedly, and for this reason the two samples could not be combined as regards level of information. Therefore the breakdowns of opinion against level of information are for the June sample only. The classifications were made according to the total number of points scored on the questions. Those who could answer all of them correctly were placed in group 1 (High); those who could answer none of them were placed in group 7 (Low). The June sample distributed itself as follows:

INFORMATION GROUP	PERCENT OF SAMPLE
1 (High)	8%
2	15
3	15
4	20
5	14
6	12
7 (Low)	16
	100%

*

Intensive Survey

The detailed report of this survey explains the method of rating respondents on level of information as follows: "During this rather lengthy interview there were numerous indications of the extent of information the respondents possessed about the various topics under consideration. It was very apparent that some people were familiar with a large number of details whereas others spoke only in extremely general terms. Hence it was possible to rate on a three-point scale the degree of information about world affairs which was evidenced in each interview. This rating was based on the entire interview and was made according to the following criteria:

"A rating of *low* was given everyone who was unfamiliar with one or more of the following general topics covered in the interview: United Nations organization,[2] atomic bomb, England, Russia. . . . Every person given this rating was actually unfamiliar with the United Nations organization; a few of them (1 percent in June and 2 percent in August) were also unfamiliar with the atomic bomb, and a very few (less than 1 percent) did not know precisely what England or Russia was. . . .

"A rating of *medium* was given everyone who was familiar with all of the topics listed above, but failed to indicate any specific information which would qualify him for the highest rating.

"A rating of *high* was given to the people who indicated a definite knowledge of world affairs by specific reference to current events such as:

> Places where recent events of importance have occurred, such as Iran, Palestine, Argentina, Spain, Egypt, India.

[2] Familiarity with the UN was tested by this question: "Have you been following the news about the United Nations organization during the last few months? As you see it, what is the main thing the UNO is set up to do?" Those who were unable to give even a very simple answer to the latter part of the question were considered to be unfamiliar with the organization.

Persons prominent in world affairs, such as Churchill, Gromyko, Molotov, Bevin, Byrnes. Mention of President Truman's name did not meet this criterion. . . .

Issues currently being discussed, such as the Russian representative's 'walking out' of the UN meetings, Stettinius' resignation, the Russian failure to withdraw troops from Iran, the veto power in the UN, the Baruch plan for international control of atomic energy.

"Approximately a third of the population falls into each of these groups."

Level of information is shown to be related to sex, age, amount of formal schooling, income, and occupation. Those who had voted in the previous national elections were as a group much higher on the informational scale than those who had not, although 21 percent of the voters were classified in the lowest information category. Some of these data are as follows:

	Rating of level of information		
	LOW	MEDIUM	HIGH
Sex			
Men	23%	34%	43%
Women	41	32	27
Education			
Some grade school	64	23	13
Complete grade school	41	35	24
Some high school	28	42	30
Complete high school	14	39	47
Some or complete college	5	33	62
Occupation			
Professional people, executives, etc.	8	30	62
Clerks, salespeople	15	28	57
Skilled workers, foremen	12	45	43
Semiskilled and unskilled workers	38	34	28
Farmers, farm workers	40	40	20
Housewives	42	33	25
Voting in 1944 Presidential election			
Voted	21	36	43
Did not vote *	51	30	19

* Not including those who were too young to vote.

Sources of Public Information

Intensive Survey

Do you have a radio here? Is it in working order?

Have radios in working order	85%
Have radios not in working order	5
Have radios, order not ascertained	1
Have no radios	9
	100%

Do you read a newspaper regularly?

Yes		83%
Daily papers only	62%	
Weekly papers only	5	
Both dailies and weeklies	16	
No		16
Not ascertained		1
		100%

Do you read any magazines regularly?

Yes		56%
One magazine	12%	
Two magazines	15	
Three	11	
Four	8	
Five	5	
Six or more	5	
No		43
Not ascertained		1
		100%

Combination of the foregoing responses shows that 80 percent have regular access to at least two of these major media:

Have three major sources of information (radio, newspapers, and magazines)		50%
Have two major sources		30
Radio and newspapers	25%	
Radio and magazines	2	
Newspapers and magazines	3	
Have only one major source		13
Radio only	8	
Newspapers only	4	
Magazines only	1	
Have none of these sources		7
		100%

Level of information is shown to be closely related to number of media available. Almost all those who are without any of the three media are in the "low" informational group; almost half those with regular access to all three media are in the "high" group. It must be understood, of course, that the better educated are far more likely than those with little education to have at hand a variety of sources, so that these figures are a reflection of differences in education as well as of differences in access to media of information.

Of those who have regularly available—	Level of information about world affairs			
	LOW	MEDIUM	HIGH	
All three sources	14%	39%	47%	100%
Two of the sources	34	34	32	100
One source only	68	26	6	100
None of the three sources	93	7	—	100

Do you listen to any radio programs where problems of world affairs are discussed? What are they?

Yes, listen to such programs		37%
Identify the specific program or programs	29%	
Do not identify specific program	8	
No, listen to no such programs		47
No, have no radios		15
Not ascertained		1
		100%

Respondents were asked whether they had heard anything about the bomb over the radio, had read about it in newspapers or magazines, had had conversations about it, had seen movies or newsreels about it. The responses were as follows:

Have heard about the bomb on the radio	81%
Have read about it in newspapers	81
Have had conversations about it	70
Have read about it in magazines	48
Have seen movies or newsreels about it	33
Have had none of these sources of information	1 *

* These questions were not asked of those who did not know what the atomic bomb is (1 percent of the sample in June, 2 percent in August).

Awareness of the Bikini Tests of the Atomic Bomb

Extensive Survey

(Asked in June, before the tests) *Do you happen to know whether there is any plan to test the atomic bomb in the near future? Will you tell me what the targets are going to be in testing the bomb?*

(Asked in August, after the tests) *Do you happen to know whether there has been any test of the atomic bomb recently? Will you tell me what targets were used in testing the bomb?*

	JUNE		AUGUST	
Knew of tests		75%		89%
Named targets correctly	63%		78%	
Named them incorrectly, or said did not know	12		11	
Did not know of tests		25		11
		100%		100%

(Asked in August, of those who had heard of the tests) *Did the atomic bombs in the recent test do more damage or less than you thought they would?*

More	13%
Same	13
Less	52
No opinion	11
	89%

Intensive Survey

Questions very similar to the foregoing were asked in the intensive survey, with very similar results. In addition, two questions were asked in June to obtain some measure of people's expectations regarding the effects of the bombs. (For those people who said they had not heard about the tests, these questions were preceded by a simple explanation of what was to be done at Bikini.)

Do you expect the bomb will destroy most of these ships, or just a few of them?

Expect great destruction	51%
Expect bombs not to be very destructive	8
Say destruction will depend on how the ships are placed, or other factors	14
Are undecided, don't know	23
Opinions not ascertained	3
Do not know what atomic bomb is	1
	100%

Do you expect the bomb to be as destructive against these ships as it was against the Japanese cities?

Yes	46%
Yes, with qualifications (e.g., "if it's the same kind of bomb")	6
No	22
Undecided, don't know	21
Opinions not ascertained	4
Do not know what atomic bomb is	1
	100%

Development of the Bomb by Other Countries

Extensive Survey

As far as you know, is the secret of how to make atomic bombs known only by the U.S., or do you think some other countries also know how to make atomic bombs?

	JUNE	AUGUST
Known only by United States	27%	30%
Known by others	60	56
No opinion	13	14
	100%	100%

On this as on many other questions, the poorly informed were more likely to have no opinions than were the better informed. When only those who expressed opinions are considered, the various informational groups are seen not to differ much in their answers, except for those at the very bottom of the informational scale:

	Level of information						
	(LOW)						(HIGH)
	7	6	5	4	3	2	1
Known only by United States	32%	32%	25%	28%	26%	22%	25%
Known by others	34	49	65	64	66	73	75
No opinion	34	19	10	8	8	5	—
	100%	100%	100%	100%	100%	100%	100%

(Omitting those with no opinion)

Known only by United States	48%	39%	28%	30%	28%	23%	25%
Known by others	52	61	72	70	72	77	75
	100%	100%	100%	100%	100%	100%	100%

(If "Known by others") *What other countries do you think know how to make atomic bombs?*

	JUNE	AUGUST
Russia	41%	41%
England	28	22
Germany	18	17
Canada	13	7
Japan	4	2
Spain	2	1
France	1	1

Various other countries were mentioned by less than 1 percent each. The percentages add to more than 60 and 56 respectively because some respondents named more than one country.

(If "Known only by U.S." or "No opinion") *How long do you think it will be before another country learns how to make atomic bombs?*

	JUNE	AUGUST
"Soon"	3%	4%
Two years or less	8	8
Three to five years	10	10
Six to ten years	4	5
More than ten years, "a long time," "will never learn"	3	2
No opinion	12	15
	40%	44%

(If "Known only by U.S." or "No opinion") *What other country do you think will learn to make atomic bombs first?*

	JUNE	AUGUST
Russia	25%	26%
England	5	5
Germany	3	5
Others	2	2
No opinion	5	6
	40%	44%

Intensive Survey

How long do you think it will be before the other countries are able to make the atomic bomb?

	JUNE	AUGUST
Some other country may already be able to	20%	24%
Not long (no precise statement of time)	16	13
Less than one year	1	3
One to three years	5	5
Three to five years	6	4
Five to ten years	5	5
Ten years or more	3	3
A long time (no precise statement of time)	3	2
No other country will be able to make it	2	2
"It depends" (no definite prediction)	8	8
Don't know	27	26
Opinions not ascertained	3	3
Do not know what atomic bomb is	1	2
	100%	100%

As in the extensive survey, the differences between poorly informed and better informed people on this question are chiefly that the former are much more likely not to have opinions.

	Level of information about world affairs					
	(All respondents)			Omitting those who express no opinion)		
	LOW	MEDIUM	HIGH	LOW	MEDIUM	HIGH
Some other country may already be able to	14%	25%	26%	35%	37%	35%
Not long	11	18	15	29	26	20
Less than three years	3	8	9	7	11	12
Three to ten years	4	11	16	10	16	22
Ten years or more; a long time	4	7	6	11	9	8
No other country will be able	3	*	2	8	1	3
"It depends"	8	8	7			
Don't know	42	21	17			
Opinions not ascertained	6	2	2			
Do not know what atom bomb is	5	—	—			
	100%	100%	100%	100%	100%	100%

* Less than 1 percent.

DEFENSE AGAINST THE BOMB

Extensive Survey

Do you think the United States will be able to work out an effective defense against the bomb before other nations could use it against us?

	JUNE	AUGUST
Yes	54%	56%
No	19	19
No opinion	27	25
	100%	100%

The poorly informed were much less likely to express opinions on this question, but when they did so they were more likely than the better informed to express faith in our ability to develop a defense. It is notable, however, that even among those at the top of the informational scale, belief in our ability to develop a defense was widespread:

Level of information

	(LOW)						(HIGH)
	7	6	5	4	3	2	1
Yes	48%	58%	55%	61%	57%	50%	41%
No	9	13	17	17	19	28	40
No opinion	43	29	28	22	24	22	19
	100%	100%	100%	100%	100%	100%	100%

(Omitting those with no opinions)

Yes	84%	82%	76%	78%	75%	64%	51%
No	16	18	24	22	25	36	49
	100%	100%	100%	100%	100%	100%	100%

Intensive Survey

Do you think we will be able to work out a defense against the bomb before other countries learn how to make it?

	JUNE	AUGUST
Yes	35%	36%
Yes, with qualifications	5	4
Undecided, don't know	36	29
No, with qualifications	1	1
No	18	24
Opinions not ascertained	4	4
Do not know what atomic bomb is	1	2
	100%	100%

	Level of information about world affairs					
	(*All respondents*)			(*Omitting those who express no opinion*)		
	LOW	MEDIUM	HIGH	LOW	MEDIUM	HIGH
Yes	29%	41%	38%	66%	60%	50%
Yes, with qualifications	4	5	4	10	8	6
Undecided, don't know	45	29	24			
No, with qualifications	*	1	1	*	1	2
No	11	21	31	24	31	42
Opinions not ascertained	6	3	2			
Do not know what atomic bomb is	5	—	—			
	100%	100%	100%	100%	100%	100%

* Less than 1 percent.

Reasons given by those who said "yes" (it should be noted that the percentages are based on the number giving this response, not on the total sample):

Since the scientists were able to invent the bomb, they can work out a defense	29%
We are working hard to develop one now	23
We will be able to keep ahead of other countries	18
A defense has always been found against weapons	10
Other reasons	3
Reasons not given	17
	100%

Reasons given by those who said "no":

There is no defense against the bomb	70%
It would take too long	11
We have not been able to work one out thus far	2
Other reasons	3
Reasons not given	14
	100%

PROSPECTS FOR AVERTING WAR

Extensive Survey

Which of these four statements comes closest to your own ideas?

	JUNE	AUGUST
I think there is bound to be another world war within the next twenty-five years	23%	25%
Things certainly are bad now, but it looks as though they will get worse, so there may be another world war within twenty-five years	24	23
Things don't look too good now, but the nations will work out ways of getting along better, so there may not be another world war within twenty-five years	40	37
I do not think there will be another world war within twenty-five years	9	11
No opinion	4	4
	100%	100%

Extreme pessimism was more common among poorly informed people, and modified optimism among the better informed:

	Level of information						
	(LOW)						(HIGH)
	7	6	5	4	3	2	1
. . . there is bound to be another war	32%	27%	23%	22%	21%	17%	10%
. . . it looks as though things will get worse, so there may be another war	23	24	22	26	23	24	28
. . . the nations will work out ways of getting along, so there may not be war	24	31	42	40	47	50	49
I do not think there will be war . . .	10	11	9	9	8	7	11
No opinion	11	7	4	3	1	2	2
	100%	100%	100%	100%	100%	100%	100%

DANGER OF ATOMIC ATTACK ON THE UNITED STATES

Extensive Survey

Do you think there is a real danger that atomic bombs will ever be used against the United States?

	JUNE	AUGUST
Yes	64%	63%
No	22	24
No opinion	14	13
	100%	100%

(If "yes" to the above question) *Do you think the danger that you or any members of your immediate family will ever be killed by an atomic bomb is very great, fairly great, or only very slight?*

	JUNE	AUGUST
Very great	8%	8%
Fairly great	21	20
Only very slight	30	29
No danger	2	2
No opinion	3	4
	64%	63%

Those who were completely optimistic about the prospects for averting war within the next twenty-five years were more likely to be optimistic about our freedom from danger of atomic at-

tack, but those whose optimism about averting war was modified did not differ much from the pessimists on this question:

*Do you think there is a real danger that atomic bombs will ever be used
against the United States?*

| | Of those who chose: | | | |
	Bound to be a war	May be war	May not be war	Will not be war
Yes	71%	71%	62%	47%
No	18	17	26	38
No opinion	11	12	12	15
	100%	100%	100%	100%

Intensive Survey

*Do you think there is a real danger that atomic bombs will ever be used
against the United States?*

	JUNE	AUGUST
Yes	17%	16%
Yes, with qualifications (mainly "if there is another war" or "if other countries get the secret") or uncertainty	46	43
Undecided, don't know	11	11
No, with qualifications or uncertainty	10	12
No	14	14
Opinions not ascertained	1	2
Do not know what atomic bomb is	1	2
	100%	100%

"WORRY" ABOUT THE BOMB

Intensive Survey

*How worried do you think people in this country are about the atomic
bomb?*

	JUNE	AUGUST
Worried, greatly worried	26%	25%
Not worried, worried very little	42	47
Some are worried, some are not	9	8
Not worried now, but would be under certain conditions	2	4
Don't know	15	11
Opinions not ascertained	5	3
Do not know what atomic bomb is	1	2
	100%	100%

How about yourself?

	JUNE	AUGUST
Greatly worried ("It worries me a lot," "Terribly worried," "I certainly am worried") Worried ("I'm worried too")	12% } 23% 11%	13% } 26% 13%
Not much worried ("Not very much," "Not too worried," "Somewhat, but not getting greyhaired over it")	11	11
Not worried ("Not at all," "I'm not worried")	54	50
Not worried now, would be under certain conditions	5	8
Don't know	2	*
Opinions not ascertained	4	3
Do not know what atomic bomb is	1	2
	100%	100%

* Less than 1 percent.

Reasons given by those who said they were worried or greatly worried (note that the percentages are of the specified group, not of the whole sample; each column may add to slightly more than 100 percent because some respondents gave more than one reason):

	Of those who said they were:	
	Greatly worried	Worried
Dangerousness of the bomb:		
The bomb is so dangerous	34%	36%
It might destroy the whole nation or the world	32	13
The bomb might get into others' hands:		
Other countries may learn how to make it; other countries might use it	20	19
Russia may learn to make it, may use it	4	4
The bomb might get into the wrong hands	5	7
Other countries know how to make it	2	—
Other reasons:		
No satisfactory control has been developed	1	3
Other	3	4
Reasons not given	10	17

Reasons given by those who said they were not worried, or very little worried:

	Of those who said they were:	
	Not much worried	Not worried
Feel secure:		
The U.S. has the bomb	6%	8%
The bomb will be outlawed	5	3
Its dangerousness has been greatly exaggerated	3	3
Other countries will not be able to make it	1	2
We can develop a defense against it	*	2
Worry is useless:		
There's nothing a person can do about it	9	14
Don't think about it; haven't time to worry about it	5	10
It is up to the leaders (or have confidence in the leaders) to handle problem	6	9
Think they themselves will never see bomb used	5	9
One has to die sometime; "wouldn't know what happened if one hit"	1	9
Other reasons:		
Don't know enough about it to worry	2	4
Have religion to look to	2	3
The bomb will benefit mankind through its peaceful uses	3	2
Other	2	5
Reasons not given	50	21

* Less than 1 percent.

Most of those who said they were not worried now, but would be under certain conditions, said they would be worried if other countries knew how to make atomic bombs.

In further analysis of the answers to the "worry" question, those who said they were not worried for reasons that indicated they thought the country safe (listed in the above table under "Feel secure") are grouped separately from those who gave reasons grouped as "worry is useless." Reasons of the latter kind were much more frequent than those of the former kind. It may be seen from the next table that level of information bore little relation to "worry," and that voters as a group admitted to neither more nor less worry than nonvoters.

	Level of information about world affairs			Voting in 1944 national election	
	LOW	MEDIUM	HIGH	VOTED	DID NOT VOTE **
Greatly worried	11%	12%	15%	13%	13%
Worried	11	13	11	13	10
Worried very little	7	15	12	11	11
Not worried—					
Because worry is useless	23	25	25	25	24
Because they feel secure	7	7	11	8	6
Other reasons, no reason given	22	18	18	20	19
Not worried now, would be under certain conditions	7	7	5	6	6
Don't know, attitudes not ascertained	6	3	3	4	6
Do not know what bomb is	6	—	—	*	5
	100%	100%	100%	100%	100%

* Less than 1 percent.
** Does not include those who were too young to vote.

As would be expected, people with optimistic opinions regarding the bomb—who said, for instance, that it would take other countries a long time to develop the bomb, that we would have a defense against it, or that there was no real danger to the United States—were less likely to say they worried about the bomb than people who were not optimistic on such questions. Nevertheless, even among those who acknowledged the menace of the bomb, only a minority said they were worried.

Do you think there is real danger that atomic bombs will ever be used against the United States?

	Of those who said:			
	Yes	Yes, with qualifica-tions	No, with qualifica-tions	No
Greatly worried	17%	14%	8%	8%
Worried	17	14	8	9
Not much worried	12	12	6	13
Not worried—				
Because worry is useless	21	24	31	26
Because they feel secure	6	7	14	12
Other reasons, no reason given	19	18	22	23
Not worried now, would be under certain conditions	4	7	11	6
Don't know, or attitudes not ascertained	4	4	—	3
	100%	100%	100%	100%

How long do you think it will be before other countries are able to make the bomb?

	Of those who said:			
	May be able to now	Not long; less than three years	Three to ten years	Ten years or more; long time; will never be able
Greatly worried	12%	19%	13%	5%
Worried	12	11	15	11
Not much worried	14	12	13	3
Not worried—				
Because worry is useless	27	25	22	24
Because they feel secure	8	5	12	22
Other reasons, no reason given	19	18	15	21
Not worried now, would be under certain conditions	4	6	7	9
Don't know, or attitudes not ascertained	4	4	3	5
	100%	100%	100%	100%

Do you think we will be able to work out a defense against the bomb before other countries learn how to make it?

	Of those who said:	
	Yes	No
Greatly worried	9%	16%
Worried	11	14
Not much worried	11	12
Not worried—		
Because worry is useless	26	26
Because they feel secure	10	9
Other reasons, no reason given	21	15
Not worried now, would be under certain conditions	8	6
Don't know, or attitudes not ascertained	4	2
	100%	100%

INTERNATIONAL CONTROL OF ATOMIC ENERGY

Extensive Survey

Do you think the secret of making atomic bombs should be put under the control of the United Nations organization, or should the United States keep the secret to itself?

	JUNE	AUGUST
The UN should control it	21%	18%
The United States should keep it	72	75
Qualified answers	2	2
No opinion	5	5
	100%	100%

The higher the respondent stood on the informational scale, the more likely he was to react favorably to the idea of UN control of the secret, but even at the top of the informational scale only a minority approved:

	Level of information						
	(LOW)						(HIGH)
	7	6	5	4	3	2	1
The UN should control it	5%	10%	15%	23%	29%	33%	37%
The United States should keep it	80	83	80	73	64	62	54
Qualified answers	1	1	1	1	3	3	8
No opinion	14	6	4	3	4	2	1
	100%	100%	100%	100%	100%	100%	100%

The next question was a broader one about international control, in which neither "secrets" nor the UN were mentioned. Only a small minority opposed international control in principle:

Which of these three statements comes closest to what you think the United States should do?

	JUNE	AUGUST
The U.S. should go on making atomic bombs, and not depend on systems of international control of the bombs	21%	22%
We should go on making atomic bombs for the time being, but try to work out a system of international control to prevent any nation, including our own, from using atomic bombs	49	47
We should stop making atomic bombs right now and try to work out a system of international control to keep other nations from making them too	25	26
No opinion	5	5
	100%	100%

Here the differences among groups differing in informedness were not so marked, although if only those who expressed opinions are considered it may be seen that there were about twice as many at the bottom of the informational scale as at the top who chose the first statement—that the United States should "not depend on systems of international control." Nevertheless, except at the bottom of the scale the opinion that "we should go on making atomic bombs for the time being" was decidedly more popular than that we should stop making them "right now."

	Level of information						
	(LOW)						(HIGH)
	7	6	5	4	3	2	1
The U.S. should go on making atomic bombs and not depend on systems of international control	26%	21%	19%	20%	21%	19%	16%
We should go on making atomic bombs for the time being, but try to work out a system of international control	30	43	53	49	57	56	62
We should stop making atomic bombs right now and try to work out a system of international control	28	29	24	28	20	22	20
No opinion	16	7	4	3	2	3	2
	100%	100%	100%	100%	100%	100%	100%

Only an insignificant proportion of those who approved of putting the secret under UN control chose the statement that the United States "should not depend on international control" in preference to the other two statements. But, like those who opposed turning the secret over, they were twice as likely to favor "going on making bombs for the time being" as they were to favor an immediate discontinuation of bomb production:

	Of those who said:	
	The UN should control secret	United States should keep it
The United States should go on making atomic bombs and not depend on systems of international control	5%	27%
We should go on making atomic bombs for the time being, but try to work out a system of international control	61	46
We should stop making atomic bombs right now and try to work out a system of international control	32	23
No opinion	2	4
	100%	100%

Although in general the better informed appear to be of a more "international" frame of mind than the poorly informed, on the question of whether international supervision and control can prevent atomic warfare, they differ only in that more of the poorly informed would venture no opinions:

Do you think a system of international supervision and control can prevent all countries from making atomic bombs and using them against each other?

	JUNE	AUGUST	Level of information						
			(LOW) 7	6	5	4	3	2	(HIGH) 1
Yes	35%	37%	27%	36%	33%	35%	35%	42%	41%
No	50	50	37	43	52	56	60	54	55
No opinion	15	13	36	21	15	9	5	4	4
	100%	100%	100%	100%	100%	100%	100%	100%	100%

Many of those who approved of turning the secret over to the UN, or at least of trying to work out a system of international control, were dubious about how effective such a system would prove to be:

Do you think a system of international supervision and control can prevent all countries from making (and using) atomic bombs. . . ?

	Of those who said:	
	The UN should control secret	United States should keep it
Yes	55%	32%
No	40	54
No opinion	5	14
	100%	100%

Do you think a system of international supervision and control can prevent all countries from making (and using) atomic bombs. . . ?

	Of those who said the U.S. should:		
	Continue making bombs, not depend on control system	Make bombs for time being, work toward control	Stop making bombs, work for control
Yes	20%	41%	43%
No	64	51	44
No opinion	16	8	13
	100%	100%	100%

Intensive Survey

In the intensive survey, the question of turning control of the secret over to the UN was put only to those people who gave evidence of knowing what the UN is. In June, these were 69 percent of the sample, in August 66 percent.

Do you think the secret of the bomb should be turned over to the UN or should the United States try to keep the secret itself?

	Of those who were familiar with UN:	
	JUNE	AUGUST
It should be turned over to the UN	15%	10%
It should be turned over to the UN under some conditions	4	5
It should be kept by the United States except under certain conditions	12	12
It should be kept by the United States	58	62
It is not a secret	3	6
Undecided, don't know	7	4
Opinions not ascertained	1	1
	100%	100%

Those who unqualifiedly approved of turning the secret over to the UN gave the following reasons (the percentages add to more than 100 because some gave more than one reason):

	Of those who said it should be turned over to the UN
The secret cannot be kept	37%
Turning it over to the UN would help keep peace	31
It would show faith in the UN	21
Atomic energy could then be used for peaceful purposes	10
Turning it over to the UN would eliminate fear of the United States	5
Other countries already have the secret	4
Otherwise there will be an atomic war	2
Other reasons	11
No reason given	10

Those who unqualifiedly favored keeping the secret in U.S. hands gave the following reasons:

	Of those who said it should be kept by the U.S.
Other countries might use the bomb	32%
It is in good hands here	26
As long as we have it, others fear us; it is a protection for us	18
It was developed in this country	8
Other countries might get the secret from UN	9
UN is not sufficiently strong to control it	7
Keeping the secret will make it harder for other countries to develop the bomb	1
Other reasons	3
No reason given	13

Other Surveys Referred to in the Text

In May 1946 the National Opinion Research Center polled a national sample on the following questions:

Do you think the world organization should pass a law and be given the power to enforce it so that no country in the world can make atomic bombs, or don't you think so?

Should pass law	72%
Should not	20
Undecided	8
	100%

(If "should pass") *If passing a law that no country can make atomic bombs meant that the United States would not only have to stop making any more, but would also have to destroy all atomic bombs now on hand, would you be for or against passing this law?*

Still for law	56%
Against	13
Undecided	3
	72%

It has been suggested that the world organization have inspectors who could search any property in any country at any time to see if anybody was making atomic bombs. All inspectors would work in teams, having one Russian, one Englishman, and one American working together. Do you think there should be such an inspection, or not?

Favor inspection	75%
Against inspection	17
Undecided	8
	100%

(If "favor inspection") *Would you be willing for these inspectors to search American property if it meant that they would find out how we make atomic bombs, or would that be going too far?*

Willing	39%
Going too far	33
Undecided	3
	75%

In April 1947, the Survey Research Center of the University of Michigan included the following questions about international control of atomic energy in an intensive survey. As in our survey, conducted by the same agency, the sample was divided into three groups on the basis of evidences of general information about world affairs. One-third of the sample appeared to be unfamiliar with the purpose of the UN, and constituted the group designated as "low" on the informational scale; these were not asked the questions quoted below. The percentages in the tables are of the remaining two-thirds of the sample, those classed as at the "medium" and the "high" levels of information:

In your opinion, should there be international control of atomic bombs and atomic energy, or should each country remain free to make its own bombs?

	Of all those familiar with UN	Level of information	
		MEDIUM	HIGH
Favor international control	37%	31%	47%
Favor international control, but with qualifications or uncertainty	9	9	11
Undecided, mixed, don't know	8	11	4
Favor leaving each country free to make bombs, but with qualifications or uncertainty	7	6	9
Favor leaving each country free to make bombs	35	40	27
Opinion not ascertained	4	3	2
	100%	100%	100%

Do you think it is possible to set up an international control system that would prevent atomic war?

	Of those familiar with UN
Yes	13%
Yes, with qualifications or uncertainty	26
Undecided, mixed, don't know	11
No, with qualifications or uncertainty	9
No	36
Opinions not ascertained	5
	100%

Most of those who thought "each country should remain free to make its own bombs" said in answer to the second question that international control would not work.

Do you think it is possible to set up an international control system that would prevent atomic war?

	Of those who said:	
	There should be international control (unqualified)	Each country should be free to make atomic bombs (unqualified)
Yes	29%	3%
Yes, with qualifications or uncertainty	45	9
Undecided, don't know	7	9
No, with qualifications or uncertainty	3	12
No	15	65
Opinions not ascertained	1	2
	100%	100%

INTERNATIONAL COOPERATION AS A PRINCIPLE

Intensive Survey

One of the first questions in the intensive survey was a completely open one designed to ascertain what principle or policy came first to people's minds when they considered our relations with the rest of the world. It may be seen from the great diversity of answers that no single principle had impressed itself on the consciousness of any large proportion of the people, but the idea of international cooperation was expressed more frequently than any one other idea. The idea of maintaining a strong military position appeared to be next in prominence.

These ideas, and some of the others expressed, are not necessarily opposed to each other, and it is pointed out in the original report that "the proportions of the people who offer each of these suggestions are undoubtedly much smaller than would be the proportions who would agree to them if they were specifically proposed."

What do you think is the best thing that the United States could do to help keep peace in the world?

	JUNE		AUGUST	
Cooperate internationally		21%		18%
Cooperate with other countries	9%		8%	
Support the United Nations	5		4	
Take leadership in international affairs	2		1	
Increase understanding through education	1		2	
Improve world trade and economy	1		1	
Turn the secret of the atomic bomb over to international control	1		1	
Stop making atomic bombs; stop using the bomb as a threat	1		*	
Work toward a system of international laws and law enforcement	*		1	
Work toward a world police force	1		*	
Help other countries by sending material aid		9		5
Be firm with other countries		4		6
Keep strong armed forces		10		11
Keep strong armed forces	9		10	
Maintain strong occupation forces	1		1	
Keep atomic bomb secret		2		3
Solve problems at home		7		6
Solve problems in this country	4		2	
Improve leadership in this country	2		1	
Improve diplomatic corps	*		1	
Provide example of democracy for others	1		2	
Let other countries solve their own problems		9		11
Isolate itself from other countries	4		5	
Not interfere in internal affairs of others	4		4	
Try to stay out of other countries' wars	*		1	
Reduce material aid to other countries	1		1	
Turn to religion		6		7
Other suggestions		9		7
Believe there is nothing the United States can do to help keep peace		2		2
Don't know		18		20
Opinions not ascertained		3		4
		100%		100%

* Less than 1 percent.

"Cooperate internationally" was an especially common answer among the well-informed. "Let other countries solve their own problems" was high on the list of suggestions made by the poorly informed:

	Level of information about world affairs		
	LOW	MEDIUM	HIGH
Cooperate internationally	10%	19%	27%
Help other countries with material aid	6	8	8
Be firm with other countries	3	6	8
Keep strong armed forces	5	15	12
Keep atomic bomb secret	2	2	5
Solve problems at home	4	7	8
Let other countries solve their own problems	11	8	9
Turn to religion	8	8	3
Other opinions	7	8	8
Don't know	38	16	10
Opinions not ascertained	6	3	2
	100%	100%	100%

When asked directly how they felt about a policy of complete isolationism, even the poorly informed gave it only minority approval:

Some people would like to see our government keep to itself and not have anything to do with the rest of the world. How would you feel about this?

	JUNE	AUGUST	Level of information about world affairs		
			LOW	MEDIUM	HIGH
Approve	8%	9%	16%	5%	4%
Approve with qualifications or uncertainty	8	5	12	4	4
Undecided, don't know	7	8	16	4	1
Disapprove, with qualifications or uncertainty	7	7	9	7	5
Disapprove	69	69	44	79	85
Opinions not ascertained	1	2	3	1	1
	100%	100%	100%	100%	100%

The explanations people gave for their attitudes on this question were as follows:

	Of those who:		
	Approved	Approved with qualifications	Disapproved with qualifications	Dis-approved
---	---	---	---	---
Such a policy would prevent our getting involved in wars	43%	12%	5%	
We should not mix in other countries' affairs	21	21	13	
Sending material help to other countries is hard on us; we should use our money and material goods at home	4	7	4	
We cannot trust other countries	4	1	2	
Trade is necessary		15	34	37%
Such a policy would be unfriendly, selfish		3	14	31
Transportation and communication have brought countries close together		1	6	16
Past experience has proved isolationism impossible		—	2	14
Such a policy is likely to cause trouble with other countries		—	2	6
We wouldn't know what was going on in other countries		—	1	5
We wouldn't be able to provide an example for others		—	1	2
Events in other countries will affect us anyway		—	1	2
Other reasons or qualifications	11	30	11	3
Reasons not given	19	29	26	8
	*	*	*	*

* Each column adds to more than 100 percent because some respondents gave more than one reason.

Responses to a series of questions about the UN indicate that a very large majority of those who were familiar with the purpose of the organization approved of it in principle, that most of them felt the United States should have no greater voice in the UN than the other large powers have, and the UN should have the power to arbitrate disputes involving the United States. On the other hand, there was only moderate optimism about the ultimate success of the organization:

How do you feel about the general idea of having an organization like the UN?

	Of those familiar with UN	
	JUNE	AUGUST
Approve	71%	65%
Approve with qualifications or uncertainty	22	24
Undecided, don't know	4	3
Disapprove with qualifications or uncertainty	1	2
Disapprove	1	3
Opinions not ascertained	1	3
	100%	100%

(The report states that "few of those shown in the table as 'approving with qualifications or uncertainty' indicate the nature of their reservations. Most of these people simply answer in an unemphatic way, as for example, 'Well, I guess it's a good idea.' ")

Do you think the United States ought to have more say than the other big countries (in the UN), or should they all have the same?

	Of those familiar with UN	
	JUNE	AUGUST
U.S. should have more say than the others	19%	27%
U.S. should probably have more say	3	2
Undecided, don't know	3	3
U.S. should probably have same say as the others	7	3
U.S. should have same say	61	59
Opinions not ascertained	7	6
	100%	100%

Reasons	Of those who said the U.S. should have "more say"
We put more into the war than the others	30%
We have sent more material help to other countries	27
We are larger, richer, stronger	15
We are in a position of moral leadership	7
We are peace-loving	6
We have no interest in acquiring more power or territory or in interfering in other countries' affairs	6
Other reasons	5
Reasons not given	4
	100%

	Of those who said the U.S. should have "the same say"
It would not be right for any country to have more voice than any other	36%
Otherwise the UN would not be what it is intended to be	20
If we had more say, there would be trouble between us and other countries	19
We all fought together in the war	1
Other reasons	3
Reasons not given	21
	100%

Suppose the United States and another country had a disagreement which they couldn't settle. Do you think the UN should have the power to tell both of them what ought to be done?

	Of those familiar with UN	
	JUNE	AUGUST
Yes	65%	68%
Yes, with qualifications or uncertainty	19	17
Undecided, don't know	4	3
No, with qualifications or uncertainty	3	1
No	3	5
Opinions not ascertained	6	6
	100%	100%

How successful do you think the UN will be in keeping peace among the countries?

	Of those familiar with UN	
	JUNE	AUGUST
Successful	6%	10%
Probably successful (qualifications, uncertainty)	38	35
Undecided, don't know	25	27
Probably unsuccessful (qualifications, uncertainty)	14	12
Unsuccessful	10	11
Opinions not ascertained	7	5
	100%	100%

By far the major qualification was "if the nations live up to their obligations, if all work together."

The two questions on world organization asked in the intensive survey are shown below in the order in which they were asked. The formulation of the first question probably influenced some people's answers to the second—that is, in considering how they felt about the participation of the United States in a world organization "where we would have to follow the decisions of the majority of the nations," many may have thought of its structure as resembling "the way the states in this country are organized."

Do you think it would be possible to organize the nations of the world in the same way the states in this country are organized, with a government over them all to make laws that they would all have to obey?

	JUNE	AUGUST
Yes, or yes with qualifications	24%	23%
Undecided, don't know	11	10
No, or no with qualifications	57	58
Opinions not ascertained	8	9
	100%	100%

Skepticism about this proposal was equally prevalent at all three levels of information, if allowance is made for differences in the proportions who "don't know."

*Level of information
about world affairs*

	LOW	MEDIUM	HIGH
Yes, or yes with qualifications	18%	25%	26%
Undecided, don't know	21	7	4
No, or no with qualifications	46	62	65
Opinions not ascertained	15	6	5
	100%	100%	100%

About a third of all those who answered "yes" gave no explanations for their opinion; by far the most prominent among the stated reasons was that "such a government has succeeded in the United States." Those who said "no" gave as their reason that "the differences among countries are too great" or that "countries aren't willing to cooperate to such an extent." The most prominent qualification was "if [or "not unless"] there were enough time to work it out."

How would you feel about this country belonging to a world organization where we would have to follow the decisions of the majority of the nations?

	JUNE	AUGUST
Approve, or approve with qualifications	41%	34%
Undecided, don't know	13	11
Disapprove, or disapprove with qualifications	39	48
Opinions not ascertained	7	7
	100%	100%

A disproportionate share of the disapproval came from the poorly informed. Among the better informed two-thirds—those who were familiar with the UN—half of those with opinions reacted favorably to the suggestion even in August.

	Of those familiar with UN	
	JUNE	AUGUST
Approve, or approve with qualifications	50%	44%
Undecided, don't know	8	7
Disapprove, disapprove with qualifications	36	43
Opinions not ascertained	6	6
	100%	100%

Reasons	Of those who approved
It is the only way to keep peace	14%
The majority should be right	14
Without the United States there would be no point in having such an organization	5
It would be like the UN	5
It is the only fair way	5
That is the way the United States is governed	4
The United States is no better than other countries	4
It would keep any one country from having too much power	1
Other reasons for approving	5
Approve on condition that:	
Such an organization proved workable	10
All countries belonged to it	5
Its decisions were fair	5
It did not interfere in the internal affairs of any country	5
It was necessary in order to keep peace	3
It had proper leadership	2
Countries would not pursue selfish interests	1
Other conditions	6
Reasons not given	16
	*

* The column adds to more than 100 percent because some respondents gave more than one reason.

	Of those who disapproved
We prefer our system of government just as it is	29%
We would not want our decisions or laws made by others	26
They might make us do something we wouldn't want to	13
Differences among countries are too great	10
The scheme would not work	6
Other countries would not be fair to the U.S.	4
Other countries cannot handle even their own affairs	2
It might provoke trouble	2
It would give the smaller nations too much voice	1
Other countries are too far behind us	1
Other reasons for disapproving	7
Reasons not given	10
	*

* The column adds to more than 100 percent because some respondents gave more than one reason.

Other Surveys Referred to in the Text

On August 1, 1946, Elmo Roper reported the following results of a national poll in his column in the *New York Herald Tribune:*

If every other country in the world would elect representatives to a world congress and let all problems between countries be decided by this congress, with a strict provision that all countries have to abide by the decisions whether they like them or not, would you be willing to have the United States go along on this?

Yes	63%
No	20
Undecided	17
	100%

If every other country in the world would turn over to a world organization all their military secrets, and allow continuous inspection, would you be willing for the United States to go along on this?

Yes	47%
No	38
Undecided	15
	100%

The American Institute of Public Opinion (Gallup Poll) reported the following question and answers in its release of August 18, 1946:

Do you think the United Nations organization should be strengthened to make it a world government with power to control the armed forces of all nations, including the United States?

Yes	54%
No	24
Undecided	22
	100%

LOANS TO FOREIGN COUNTRIES

Intensive Survey

In June of 1946, when interviewing for the first section of the survey was going on, the loan to Britain was being debated in Congress. By August, it had received Congressional approval.

(Asked in June) *There's talk now about the United States lending a large amount of money to England. How do you feel about that?*

(Asked in August) *You probably know that Congress recently voted to lend a large amount of money to England. How do you feel about that?*

	JUNE	AUGUST
Approve	10%	18%
Approve with qualifications or uncertainty	28	19
Undecided, don't know	13	12
Disapprove with qualifications or uncertainty	8	8
Disapprove	40	42
Opinions not ascertained	1	1
	100%	100%

The report points out that "it is apparent from the reasons people give to explain their stand regarding the loan that a relatively small part of the population has any understanding of the actual purposes of the loan. Only about one-third of the small proportion who fully support it mention its economic advantages to this country or to the world in general through its effect on trade, and among the other groups. . . . there is almost no mention of the relation between the loan and foreign trade." Three considerations were outstanding in people's reactions to the question: the ability of the United States to make the loan, England's failure to repay the previous loan, England's need for the money. The tabulation of reasons given follows:

	Of those who:			
	Approved	Approved with qualifications	Disapproved with qualifications	Disapproved
Reasons for approval:				
They need the money	49%	22%	7%	
It will help our foreign trade or world trade	35	9	4	
It will insure England's friendship	14	5	—	
We fought together in the war	9	1	1	
We have traditional ties with her	2	2	—	
It will help keep peace	2	2	—	
Other reasons	4	1	1	

	Of those who:			
	Approved	Approved with quali- fications	Disapproved with qualifica- tions	Disap- proved
Conditions for approval:				
If England really needs the loan		18	2	
If we make sure it will be repaid		17	13	
If it is a sound financial arrangement		14	10	
If we have enough money for our own needs		11	2	
If it is a smaller loan		6	9	
If we have some control over how the money is spent		4	1	
If the needy in other countries are cared for first		2	—	
If it will help keep peace		2	—	
If it promotes world trade or economic stability		1	—	
Other conditions		5	2	
Reasons for disapproval:				
They owe us too much; it will not be repaid		17	40	55%
It will be hard on us eco- nomically		2	28	42
We have done enough for the English		2	8	16
They may use the money in an unfriendly way		1	1	4
They do not need it (as much as others)		*	10	11
It may cause trouble when (if) we try to collect		1	—	3
They may use the money to our disadvantage econom- ically		—	1	2
England has only selfish in- terests		1	2	2
Other reasons		*	4	5
Reasons not given	9	10	11	4
	**	**	**	**

* Less than 1 percent.
** Each column adds to more than 100 percent because some respondents offered more than one comment.

Even a direct question implying that the United States might gain from the loan elicited relatively little recognition of its possible economic benefits to us:

Do you think we have anything to gain from making the loan?

	JUNE	AUGUST
Yes, England's friendship	18%	22%
Yes, improvement in world or American trade or business	16	14
Yes, interest on the money	2	2
Yes, the loan is an aid to peace	1	1
Yes, other or unspecified gains	1	2
No	40	40
Don't know	17	15
Opinions not ascertained	5	4
	100%	100%

A proposal to lend money to Russia drew even less support:

There's talk now about the United States lending a large amount of money to Russia. How do you feel about that?

	JUNE	AUGUST
Approve	7%	6%
Approve with qualifications or uncertainty	22	16
Undecided, don't know	11	10
Disapprove with qualifications or uncertainty	14	12
Disapprove	44	53
Opinions not ascertained	2	3
	100%	100%

To quote again from the report: "Even among those who favor lending to Russia, an extremely small proportion refer to the effect of such a loan on our trade or world trade. The desirability of the loan is judged on entirely different bases: 1) Russia's friendship for this country . . . 2) Russia's need for the loan . . . 3) our economic ability to make a large loan." The reasoning accompanying the questions is tabulated as follows:

	Of those who:			
	Approved	Approved with qualifications	Disapproved with qualifications	Disapproved
Reasons for approval:				
They need the money	26%	6%	1%	
We should be as willing to lend to one ally as to another	25	7	—	
It will insure Russia's friendship	21	7	*	
It will help U.S. or world trade	19	4	*	
We fought together in the war	16	5	*	
Russia will repay it	14	6	2	
It will help keep peace	4	2	—	
Other reasons	8	1	*	
Conditions for approval:				
If Russia really needs the loan		18	4	
If Russia shows she will be friendly		13	29	
If we lend to England		13	9	
If we have enough money for our own needs		11	4	
If it is a sound financial arrangement		10	4	
If we have some control over how the money is spent		6	5	
If it is a smaller loan		5	3	
If we make sure it will be repaid		4	—	
If it will help keep peace		3	3	
If it promotes world trade or economic stability		1	—	
Other conditions		8	6	
Reasons for disapproval:				
They may use it in an unfriendly way		3	15	33%
They do not need it		3	11	26
It will be hard on us economically		3	15	21
Russia is not cooperating (or not friendly) with the United States		*	7	16
It will not be repaid		3	6	15

	Of those who:			
	Approved	Approved with qualifications	Disapproved with qualifications	Disapproved
We have done enough for Russia		1	5	9
They don't need it as much as others		—	3	2
Russia has only selfish interests		—	*	3
They may use the money to our economic disadvantage		—	1	*
Other reasons		—	3	3
Reasons not given	3	5	9	4
	**	**	**	**

* Less than 1 percent.
** Each column adds to more than 100 percent because some respondents made more than one comment.

Do you think we have anything to gain from making the loan?

	JUNE	AUGUST
Yes, Russia's friendship	20%	17%
Yes, improvement in world or American trade or business	10	4
Yes, interest on the money	1	1
Yes, other or unspecified gains	2	3
No	46	58
Don't know	14	12
Opinions not ascertained	7	5
	100%	100%

People's attitudes toward the loans were of course closely related to their general feelings toward the respective countries. (See "Attitudes Toward England and Russia," below.) Nevertheless, in spite of prevailingly friendly feelings toward England, the most common combination of opinions on the two loan questions was that we should lend to neither country. Only one person in seven (in August) said we should lend to both countries, and the degree to which a British loan was favored over a Russian loan was not so great as might perhaps be expected.

15% approved of loans to both countries (including those who expressed this opinion with qualifications or uncertainty).

27% took a more favorable (or less unfavorable) view of lending to England than of lending to Russia.

13% took a more favorable (or less unfavorable) view of lending to Russia than of lending to England.

41% disapproved of lending to either country.

4% were undecided about loans to both countries.*

* Respondents who were "undecided" about a loan to one country but favorable toward a loan to the other were counted as being more favorable toward the latter; those who were undecided about one but unfavorable toward the other were counted as being more favorable (less unfavorable) toward the former.

Other Surveys Referred to in the Text

A *Fortune* survey reported in the issue of March 1947:

If we can't do both at the same time, which do you think we should do first:

See that our military forces are kept at about their present strength, or balance the national budget?

Keep up forces	71%
Balance budget	17
Express no opinion	12

Continue to send food to needy countries, or balance the national budget?

Send food	56%
Balance budget	31
Express no opinion	13

Reduce taxes, or balance the national budet?

Reduce taxes	33%
Balance budget	53
Express no opinion	14

Continue making loans to foreign nations, or balance the national budget?

Continue loans	14%
Balance budget	70
Express no opinion	16

Attitudes toward England and Russia

Intensive Survey

The original report of the intensive survey states that "one-fifth of the people interviewed mentioned England spontaneously, before any questions about that country were raised by the interviewer. Nearly half these people made comments in which neither approval nor disapproval of England was indicated. The others almost without exception expressed criticism of England. In June, the most frequent criticisms made in this way were that England expects too much aid from the United States, and that she is seeking power. In August, specific disapproval of the loan to England, which had already been approved by Congress, was expressed most frequently. Criticisms of England's handling of the Palestine situation and comments about her failure to pay her debts to the United States were also more frequent among the spontaneous comments in August."

Do you think the English Government is trying to cooperate with the rest of the world as much as it can?

	JUNE	AUGUST	Level of information about world affairs		
			LOW	MEDIUM	HIGH
Yes, or yes with qualifications	33%	31%	22%	39%	35%
Undecided, don't know	22	23	48	11	8
No, or no with qualifications	42	43	25	47	56
Opinions not ascertained	3	3	5	3	1
	100%	100%	100%	100%	100%

The report points out that the explanations people offered for these opinions "indicate their general conception of England, for the most part, rather than approval or disapproval of specific acts or utterances of the English Government. That nearly half the people who say England is being cooperative offer no reasons to substantiate that opinion suggests that in many cases this answer is based simply on friendly or optimistic feelings."

Reasons	Of those who said: Yes, or yes with quali- fications	No, or no with quali- fications
England is trying to bring about peace	13%	
She has taken steps to give her colonies their independence	8	
She is cooperating in the UN and peace conferences	7	
She has given up food to send to others	3	
She sees that it is in her own interest to cooperate	2	
Other reasons for believing that England is trying to cooperate	9	
England wants as much power as she can get, is imperialistic	6	55%
She exploits her colonies	3	13
She has mishandled the Palestine situation	2	11
She expects too much help from the United States	2	8
She is stirring up unrest in other countries	*	5
She never pays her debts	—	3
She is not helping in the relief of Europe	—	1
Other reasons for believing that England is not trying to cooperate	2	8
England is cooperating as long as it is to her advantage to do so	4	5
She is cooperating only with the United States	*	2
She is cooperating as much as she can in her present economic condition	1	—
She is cooperating as much as she can as an imperialist power	3	1
She cooperates as long as other countries "give in" to her	1	1
Reasons not given	48	11
	**	**

* Less than 1 percent.
** Each column adds to more than 100 percent because some respondents made more than one comment.

In spite of the widespread opinion that the English Government was not being as cooperative as it should, only a small
proportion of the people felt that the United States could not
count on England's friendship:

*How about the United States? Do you think we can count on the English
Government being friendly with us?*

	JUNE	AUGUST	Level of information about world affairs		
			LOW	MEDIUM	HIGH
Yes	41%	48%	23%	49%	61%
Yes, with qualifications or un-certainty	30	20	24	31	21
Undecided, don't know	14	15	32	6	3
No, with qualifications or un-certainty	8	9	9	9	8
No	5	7	8	4	6
Opinions not ascertained	2	1	4	1	1
	100%	100%	100%	100%	100%

On the question of whether the English Government is
cooperating, the well-informed showed themselves to be more
critical of England than the poorly informed, but they were
more confident, nevertheless, that the United States can count
on England's friendship.

Reasons	Yes	Yes, with qualifications	No	No, with qualifications
We can count on it because:				
She has traditional ties with the U.S.	42%	11%	1%	
She depends on us to help her	30	8	2	
She recognizes the help we gave her during the war	11	8	4	
We fought together in the war	7	2	—	
It is in her own interest militarily to remain friendly	6	1	—	
She knows we are stronger than she	4	2	1	
Other reasons	7	2	—	
We can count on it if, or cannot unless:				
It is in her interest to be friendly		34	52	
We make the loan to her		5	4	
Other conditions		10	8	
We cannot count on it (or there is reason for uncertainty) because:				
She cannot be trusted		—	5	25%
She wants as much power as she can get		4	10	21
She never pays her debts		1	5	7
She is not grateful for the help we gave during the war		*	1	7
She is our economic competitor		1	—	1
Other reasons **		2	8	22
Reasons not given	8	26	20	21
	***	***	***	***

Above columns headed: *Of those who said:*

* Less than 1 percent.

** "These represent references to specific acts of unfriendliness in the distant past ('she turned on us once') or to recent acts or utterances interpreted as unfriendly, such as Churchill's speech in Missouri."

*** The columns each add to more than 100 percent because some respondents gave more than one reason.

More than half those who thought England was trying to cooperate with the rest of the world approved of the British loan (with or without qualifications), whereas among those who said she was not trying to cooperate only about a quarter approved of the loan. Opinion about the loan was even more closely related to opinion about whether our government could depend on England's friendship:

	Do you think we can count on the English Government being friendly with us?			
	Of those who said:			
How do you feel about (the British loan)?	Yes	Yes, with qualifications	No, with qualifications	No
Approve	27%	7%	2%	—
Approve with qualifications or uncertainty	25	27	11	4
Undecided, don't know	7	11	7	4
Disapprove with qualifications or uncertainty	8	11	8	7
Disapprove	32	43	72	85
Opinions not ascertained	1	1	—	—
	100%	100%	100%	100%

The questions asked about England were also asked regarding Russia. The original report states that "half the people in the survey made comments about Russia before any questions about that country were raised by the interviewer, whereas only a fifth mentioned England in this way. Only rarely were the spontaneous remarks about Russia favorable; most of the comments had to do with disagreements between Russia and the United States or were charges of uncooperativeness or undue desire for power on Russia's part. (There was little difference between the comments made in June and those in August.)"

The Survey Research Center incorporated into an intensive survey in December 1946 two questions about Russia identical with those it had asked in our intensive survey. The December results are therefore also quoted.

How about Russia? Do you think the Russian Government is trying to cooperate with the rest of the world as much as it can?

	JUNE	AUGUST	DECEMBER
Yes	3%	2%	4%
Yes, with qualifications or uncertainty	10	7	15
Undecided, don't know	14	15	14
No, with qualifications or uncertainty	21	12	24
No	49	61	42
Opinions not ascertained	3	3	1
	100%	100%	100%

The table of reason (based on the June and August samples) is of interest as much because of the infrequency of certain statements (e.g., "Russia is fostering communism in other countries") as because of the frequency of others. Of course many people who do not volunteer a particular statement in answer to such an open question as, "Why do you think so?" would concur in it, but a very low frequency is nevertheless significant:

	Of those who said:		
Reasons	Yes, or yes with qualifications *	No, with qualifications	No
Russia does not want war	8%	4%	
She has given in on some issues	7	3	
She cooperated with us in the war	4	1	
She is trying to help the smaller countries	2	1	
Other reasons for believing she is trying to cooperate	11		
Russia wants to increase her power, and will do anything to that end	3	16	43%
She disagrees with other countries	1	24	27
She has not cooperated in UN or peace conferences	3	5	17
She does not want anyone to know what is going on in Russia	—	3	7
She has acted in an unfriendly way to the United States	1	1	5
She is fostering communism in other countries	1	1	4

Reasons	Of those who said:		
	Yes, or yes with quali-fications *	No, with qualifi-cations	No
She has a fundamentally different form of government and cannot get along with others	1	2	4
She is suspicious of others	5	3	4
She has not kept her promises	—	2	2
She is trying to increase her own security	2	3	1
She wants the secret of the atomic bomb	1	—	1
She is suspicious of the Anglo-American alliance	2	—	1
Other reasons for believing she is not trying to cooperate	4	7	6
She is cooperating as long as she has her own way about everything	4	10	
She will cooperate as long as she fears capitalist countries	2	—	
Other qualifications	17	11	
Reasons not given	43	28	5
	**	**	**

* The number in the sample who answered with an unqualified "yes" was too small for separate analysis.

** Each column adds to more than 100 percent because some respondents made more than one comment.

Do you think we can count on the Russian Government being friendly with us?

	JUNE	AUGUST	DECEMBER
Yes, yes with qualifications	36%	25%	39%
Undecided, don't know	18	16	17
No, no with qualifications	44	57	43
Opinions not ascertained	2	2	1
	100%	100%	100%

The opinion that we could count on Russia was more common among the better informed than among the poorly informed; but the shift between June and August resulted in a considerable change in the balance of opinion among the better informed:

Do you think we can count on the Russian Government being friendly with us?

	Level of information					
	Low		*Medium*		*High*	
	JUNE	AUG.	JUNE	AUG.	JUNE	AUG.
Yes, yes with qualifications	22%	15%	42%	31%	42%	31%
Undecided	33	29	12	7	9	10
No, no with qualifications	41	51	45	61	48	59
Opinions not ascertained	4	5	1	1	1	*
	100%	100%	100%	100%	100%	100%

* Less than 1 percent.

Such confidence as there was regarding the intentions of the Russian Government was displayed almost entirely by people who had similarly favorable feelings regarding England. In August,

- 22% said we could count on both England's and Russia's friendship.
- 54% took a more favorable (or less unfavorable) view of the dependability of England's friendship than of Russia's.
- 6% took a more favorable (or less unfavorable) view of the dependability of Russia's friendship than of England's.*
- 11% thought we could count on neither country.
- 7% were undecided about both countries.

* Included here are 3 percent who said we could count on Russia but not on England, 2 percent who said we could count on Russia but were undecided about England, 1 percent who were undecided about Russia but said we could not count on England. In each case those who were undecided about one country but favorable to the other were counted as being more favorable to the latter.

People's feelings about England's intentions bore no relation to their opinions about whether there was any danger that atomic bombs might some time be used against the United States; but they were somewhat more likely to acknowledge such a danger if they had said we could not count on Russia than if they had said we could:

Do you think there is real danger that atomic bombs will ever be used against the United States?

	Of those who said (with or without qualifications) that the United States:			
	Can count on England	Cannot count on England	Can count on Russia	Cannot count on Russia
Yes, yes with qualifications	64%	60%	55%	68%
Undecided, don't know	8	11	7	11
No, no with qualifications	27	27	37	20
Opinions not ascertained	1	2	1	1
	100%	100%	100%	100%

The intercorrelation of these views is not nearly so great as might be expected, however, a fact that points to the tentativeness of many of the opinions expressed. In the original report, following a more detailed exploration, the statement is made that "it is apparent throughout this study that a relatively small proportion of the public has worked out a consistent and detailed point of view on world problems. Some people seemed to be facing these problems for the first time in the interview; some appeared to hold certain general beliefs which seemed independent of each other."

People who were skeptical of the friendliness of the other major powers were somewhat less likely to be favorable toward world organization than those who thought we could count on their friendship:

How would you feel about the United States belonging to a world organization where we would have to follow the decisions of the majority of the nations?

	Of those who said (with or without qualifications) that the United States:			
	Can count on England	Cannot count on England	Can count on Russia	Cannot count on Russia
Approve, or approve with qualifications	43%	30%	48%	35%
Undecided, don't know	9	11	11	9
Disapprove, disapprove with qualifications	42	55	35	50
Opinions not ascertained	6	4	6	6
	100%	100%	100%	100%

Extensive Survey

With which one of these four statements do you come closest to agreeing?

	JUNE	AUGUST
It is very important to keep on friendly terms with Russia, and we should make every effort to do so	14%	13%
It is important for the United States to be on friendly terms with Russia, but not so important that we should make too many concessions to her	50	50
If Russia wants to keep on friendly terms with us, we shouldn't discourage her, but there is no reason why we should make any special effort to be friendly	18	17
We shall be better off if we have just as little as possible to do with Russia	14	16
No opinion	4	4
	100%	100%

Although the first statement was as infrequently chosen by well-informed as by poorly informed people, that the well-informed on the whole attached greater importance to friendly relations with Russia may be seen from the way in which their choices were distributed over the other three statements:

	Level of information						
	(Low)						(High)
	7	6	5	4	3	2	1
It is very important . . . we should make every effort	16%	16%	15%	15%	14%	11%	17%
It is important, but not so important that we should make too many concessions	24	35	46	52	60	69	65
No reason why we should make any special effort	18	20	20	19	21	15	14
Have just as little as possible to do with Russia	29	24	15	12	4	5	3
No opinion	13	5	4	2	1	—	1
	100%	100%	100%	100%	100%	100%	100%

These attitudes are seen to have a bearing upon opinions regarding UN control of the bomb secret and the efficacy of international control, although even among those who attached the greatest importance to friendly relations with Russia only a minority reacted favorably to the question about UN control:

	Of those who chose:			
	We should make every effort	Important but not too many concessions	No reason for special effort	Have as little as possible to do with Russia
UN should control the secret of atomic bomb *	32%	22%	12%	7%
United States should keep it	60	72	82	87
Qualified answers	3	3	2	1
No opinion	5	3	4	5
	100%	100%	100%	100%
International control can prevent atomic attack *	48%	38%	35%	28%
International control cannot prevent atomic attack	36	54	55	51
No opinion	16	8	10	21
	100%	100%	100%	100%

* For the phrasing of these questions, see page 113 and page 116.

CURRENT INTERNATIONAL RELATIONS AND UNITED STATES POLICIES

Intensive Survey

The following question was asked in both sections of our intensive survey and also in a similar survey conducted by the Survey Research Center in December 1946:

Now that the war is over, how do you feel about the way the countries of the world are getting along?

	JUNE	AUGUST	DECEMBER
Satisfied, mainly satisfied	16%	15%	32%
Undecided, don't know	9	9	9
Dissatisfied, mainly dissatisfied	64	71	57
Opinions not ascertained *	11	5	2
	100%	100%	100%

* "Most of the failure in ascertaining opinions on this question was due to the fact that some people would talk only about the United States—its actions in regard to other countries, or its position in international affairs."

The explanations respondents gave for their feelings on this question are summarized (as regards June and August) in the original report as follows: "Half the 'satisfied' group give no reason for their attitude, whereas all but a fifth of those who are dissatisfied offer explanations for their dissatisfaction. Such reasons as are given in support of the optimistic view are meager and general, such as that the countries are 'working for peace' or simply that they are not at war. Some who are in general satisfied, however, qualify their answers in various ways, such as 'except for Russia,' 'except for the situation in Palestine.' The most common reason given for dissatisfaction is that the nations cannot agree, that they are bickering, that they distrust one another, that each is pursuing its own ends. More than half the people who are dissatisfied make such charges. . . . One-fourth of the people who are dissatisfied refer to disagreements between Russia and other countries, and most of these blame Russia. . . ."

The following question was asked only of those who gave evidence of understanding what the UN is:

How satisfied are you with the way the UN has worked out so far?

	Of those familiar with UN	
	JUNE	AUGUST
Satisfied	10%	12%
Satisfied, with qualifications or uncertainty	33	32
Undecided, don't know	15	14
Dissatisfied, with qualifications or uncertainty	15	15
Dissatisfied	23	23
Opinions not ascertained	4	4
	100%	100%

"The people who express some degree of satisfaction appear
to divide into different types; some are well-informed people
who understand the difficulties implicit in international organization and are inclined to excuse delays, others have not followed the progress of the UN as closely and are inclined to say
it has been progressing satisfactorily inasmuch as they cannot
think of any specific criticisms."

Reasons	Of those who said they were:			
	Satis-fied	Satisfied, with quali-fications	Dissatisfied, with quali-fications	Dis-satis-fied
It has been able to settle some problems	38%	11%	1%	
It has made a real effort to settle problems	21	5	—	
It has prevented war so far	7	3	—	
Other reasons for satisfaction	5	1	—	
Greater progress could not be expected because:				
It takes time to work out something like this		22	14	
Many different nations are involved		2	1	
Other reasons		1	1	
It has not been able to accomplish anything		1	36	46%
The nations cannot agree		2	28	34
It has not been successful in handling Russia's opposition		17	15	15
The big powers are trying to force their ideas on others		*	2	4
Other reasons for dissatisfaction		2	1	7
Reasons not given	34	43	17	8
	**	**	**	**

* Less than 1 percent.
** Each column adds to more than 100 percent because some respondents gave more than one reason.

People's reactions to the question of whether England and Russia are trying to cooperate with the rest of the world (see page 136) stand in interesting contrast to their reactions to the following question regarding the behavior of the United States toward the rest of the world; it should be noted that most of those who were dissatisfied did not charge the United States with uncooperativeness.

How satisfied are you with the way the United States has been getting along with other countries since the war ended?

	JUNE	AUGUST	Level of information		
			LOW	MEDIUM	HIGH
Satisfied, mainly satisfied	60%	61%	61%	64%	55%
Undecided, don't know	9	8	19	5	4
Dissatisfied, mainly dissatisfied	26	26	14	26	37
Opinions not ascertained	5	5	6	5	4
	100%	100%	100%	100%	100%

Reasons	Of those who were:	
	Satisfied, mainly satisfied	Dissatisfied, mainly dissatisfied
The U.S. is trying to get along on a peaceful basis with other countries	34%	1%
We are helping other countries with food and other material aid	12	*
We are taking part in UN and other international organizations	1	—
We are taking a position of leadership in the world	1	—
We are handling our part of the occupation well	1	—
We have been too lenient—		
With other countries (in general)	2	14
With Russia	2	11
In our occupation policy	*	2
We are sending too much food, clothing, etc.—		
To other countries (in general)	3	16
To England	1	5
To Russia	*	1
We are not getting along with Russia	7	10
We have not handled our foreign policy adequately	1	10
We have no adequate foreign policy	—	5
We have interfered too much in internal affairs of other countries	*	5
We have not followed a consistent policy—		
Toward Argentina	*	2
Toward Spain	*	1
We have been too friendly with England	*	2
We have failed to take a position of leadership	—	2
We are not sending enough material aid abroad	*	1
Other reasons	3	12
Reasons not given	40	16
	**	**

* Less than 1 percent.
** Each column adds to more than 100 percent because some respondents gave more than one reason.

The next question followed directly after the one above in the interview. According to the report, "People who have expressed criticisms in answer to the first question were likely not to repeat them . . . others answered with different criticisms."

Do you think the United States has made any mistakes in dealing with other countries since the end of the war? What?

	JUNE	AUGUST
Yes, in actions toward specific countries:		
Has been too lenient with Russia	11%	12%
Has been too firm with Russia	1	*
Has sent too much food, clothing, etc. to Russia	1	1
Has not tried to get along with Russia	1	1
Has been too friendly with England	4	2
Has sent too much food, clothing, etc. to England	3	5
Has not followed a consistent policy toward Argentina	2	1
Has not followed a consistent policy toward Spain	1	*
Has interfered too much in China	2	1
Has not carried out an adequate occupation policy in Germany and/or Japan	5	3
Yes, in actions toward other countries in general:		
We have sent too much material help abroad	13	10
We have been too lenient with other countries	3	6
We have interfered too much in internal affairs of other countries	1	2
We have not worked out an adequate foreign policy or are not carrying it out adequately	3	1
We have failed to take a position of leadership in foreign affairs	1	1
We have not done all we could to acquire bases outside this country	1	*
Yes, in keeping the secret of the atomic bomb	1	—
Other	7	5
Yes, but don't know what the mistakes are	9	11
No, the United States has not made mistakes in dealing with other countries	25	30
Don't know	17	16
Opinions not ascertained	3	2
	**	**

* Less than 1 percent.
** Each column adds to more than 100 percent because some respondents made more than one comment.

Twenty percent made the charge, in answer to one or the other of the two questions, that the United States had been "too lenient" with other countries, and about the same proportion said we had sent too much material aid abroad.

Other Surveys Referred to in the Text

The American Institute of Public Opinion (Gallup Poll) reported the following findings on March 28 and April 13, 1947:

Do you think the problem of aid to Greece and Turkey should be turned over to the United Nations Organization?

	March 28, 1947	April 13, 1947
Yes	56%	63%
No	25	23
No opinion	19	14
	100%	100%

But in an intensive survey conducted during April 1947, the Survey Research Center asked an open question bearing upon the same point of the two-thirds of a national sample that showed themselves to be familiar with the UN:

Do you think the United States has been taking its problems to the United Nations Organization as much as it should, or do you think we have been trying to work by ourselves too much?

	Of those familiar with UN
As much as it should	52%
Undecided, don't know	22
Working alone too much	20
Opinions not ascertained	6
	100%